UP ON GAME

FROM ROBBING BANKS TO STACKING BITCOIN

Up on Game, the title of this book, signifies that someone is giving
you knowledge (game) so you become enlightened on the subject.

UP ON GAME

FROM ROBBING BANKS TO STACKING BITCOIN

*my involvement with gangs, bank robbery, prison—
and success in the business world*

RICHARD STANLEY

MELROSE
& MAIN
PUBLISHING

San Diego, CA

Trademarks of products, services, and organizations mentioned herein belong to their respective owners and are not affiliated with the publisher, Melrose & Main Publishing, LLC.

Disclaimer: The people and events portrayed in this book are real and true to the best of my memory. But to protect some people (and myself), I have changed names and left out identifying detail because cops will read this book. I hope they do. This is real life. I'm just protecting some people from harm inside and outside the system. I'm also not incriminating myself because I've done the time already. My life is my life. I don't need to embellish any facts here. They speak for themselves. Don't sue me because I can afford high-powered lawyers this time.

I am not a financial advisor and don't pretend to be one. I discuss my current business ventures as an entrepreneur in escort services and cryptocurrency. I'm not giving you business or financial advice.

Donovan prison kitchen photo courtesy Bloomberg/Getty Images.

Donovan prison cell photo courtesy KPBS, San Diego.

Cover design by Lou Anne Baker, LA Design Co.

Melrose & Main Publishing, LLC
www.UpOnGameBook.com
@UpOnGameBook
#UpOnGameBook

Paperback ISBN: 978-1-7321417-1-1
ePub ISBN: 978-1-7321417-3-5
Kindle ISBN: 978-1-7321417-2-8
Library of Congress Cataloging Number: 2018938051
Cataloging in Publication Data on file with publisher.

Printed in the United States of America.

10   9   8   7   6   5   4   3   2   1

TO MY FAMILY

CONTENTS

RICHARD'S PLAYLIST

Growing up, I collected gangster CDs—a different song for about every mood. Something to reflect on, something to get pumped up on, some hustler shit, and some party shit. Music from people who had gone through something similar as I had and came out on top. I love an underdog story. The notes included next to each song are simply the message I heard through the song or saw in the music videos. Others may take something else away.

I Got 5 on It
THE LUNIZ
(about collecting money for a marijuana purchase)

Changes
2PAC
(about neighborhood struggle/system suppression)

On My Block
SCARFACE
(about neighborhood life in general, system suppression)

Work Hard, Play Hard
WIZ KHALIFA
(the title says it all)

Refuse to Lose
BROTHA LYNCH
(about not backing down from a fight)

Masters of War
BOB DYLAN
(about the coldness of the system)

Rx (Medicate)
THEORY OF A DEADMAN
(about the abuse of prescription drugs)

Hotel California
THE EAGLES *(I say prison)*

Under the Bridge
RED HOT CHILI PEPPERS *(about the use of heroin)*

The First Day of School
ICE CUBE *(about the stripping out process and what one can expect when first getting to prison)*

Lil' Homies
2PAC *(about the reckless and dangerous nature of teenage gangsters)*

It's Going Down
CELLY CEL *(about a day in the hood)*

Gangstas Don't Live That Long
SCARFACE *(about anger at the system/venting)*

Tha Crossroads
BONE THUGS-N-HARMONY *(about death)*

So Many Tears
2PAC *(about death, hood life, prison, strife)*

Wanna Be a Baller
LIL TROY *(about wanting to get rich, but not wanting to do it illegally)*

For the Love of Money
BONE THUGS/EAZY E *(about hustling the wrong way and accepting the consequences when things happen)*

1
WE GOTTA HIT A BANK, I'M HUNGRY

SO MY FRIEND Ned and I had just acquired a newer model, gray Mitsubishi Eclipse. It was parked nearby Ned's house on a secluded stretch of side street. We had contacted a potential buyer and were just waiting for him to come by and check it out.

It was April 2002. Otay, California. I was eighteen years old.

Ned and I were playing a friendly game of Halo when hunger eventually set in. We decided to buy a grande combo meal from Taco Bell along with a two-liter Pepsi to get us through the day. We began to gather the needed funds for our planned feast and quickly realized we had only six dollars between the two of us. The meal and two liter would have cost just under ten.

I don't remember exactly what was going through my head, but I blurted out the first solution to our problem I could think of: "We should hit a bank, homie." I'm not sure if he was testing me just to see if I'd back down from my own suggestion or not, but he agreed surprisingly fast: "Fuck it, let's do it."

That was it. I realized neither of us would back down. Not now that we had both spoken on it. But I'd been waiting for a moment like this for at least four years. Boosting jewelry and candy during grade school and middle school was small time.

I grew up the same way a lot of Americans do—surrounded with gangs, drugs, violence, and poverty. My neighborhood,

Otay, pronounced (*OH-tie*)—located immediately north of the Otay Valley Regional Park area in San Diego—is only a couple miles north of Tijuana, Mexico. If you yourself are from San Diego, you may know it as the area where the bodies and body parts seem to be always turning up in the weedy riverbed.

Growing up in an environment like this as a child was a little stressful. I remember watching commercials and TV shows that would feature families in these huge homes all happy and shit, living with no worries, and I would just want that for me and my family so badly.

I also enjoyed watching informative channels such as Discovery, The Learning Channel, and even PBS. One of my favorite shows *The FBI Files* aired on Discovery most evenings. Episodes would feature different stories from different criminal cases each night. Each episode covered two to three separate cases, and each episode ended the same way: The bad guy gets caught.

I'm sure this show was intended not only for entertainment purposes, but also as a deterrent for any would-be criminals. However, I personally enjoyed the knowledge I retained from each episode. Their favorite criminals to feature were serial bank robbers and armored truck bandits. They spilled game (gave knowledge) by the gallon, and my young mind soaked it right up. They did this by breaking down each robbery step-by-step and explaining exactly what the suspect did wrong, with great detail.

I learned about law enforcement procedures immediately following a bank robbery and what the Feds would look for. The episodes covered the most common getaway routes for bank robbers, what vehicles they used, what the latest tracking devices were for the stolen loot, and where those devices could be located for removal. All from a braggy TV show.

I wasn't going to make the same mistakes the stars of the show had made. I would learn from them. Now it was time to use the free game I had received and apply it in a real way.

My parents, Tammy and Manuel, tried their best to keep me on a straight, honest path. In the nineties, my mother, a government employee, and my dad, a local truck driver, did all they could to provide for me and my sisters by regularly working sixteen-hour days. My sisters came into the picture in 1994 (Alexis) and 2000 (Veronica). By all accounts I had a well-structured home with hard-working, honest parents who clearly wanted nothing but the best for my sisters and me.

A few months after my parents had Alexis, their work hours grew longer. Whenever they had a chance for some overtime, they took it. There was no such thing as extra money—we needed it, desperately. I was still in grade school and unable to help much with babysitting duties.

A new addition to our family meant more room and more money was needed, ASAP. We soon moved to a bigger apartment in a more affordable section of the neighborhood.

Affordable and safe usually don't go hand in hand—at least where we lived. We ended up in a complex on Orange Avenue and Hilltop, walking distance from my school. My aunt was able to move in for bits of time to help with the babysitting, but not for free, and I would fill in when possible. Again, my parents were clearly doing everything they could to provide for us.

Not only were they providers, but very strict as well. My mom would warn me, "Don't be out past this time. Do your homework. Don't go play where they find the bodies. THEY'LL KILL YOU!"

To further add to their stress and worries, I fucked up in school regularly. I hated it, passionately. Despite that, I would still make my way there every day I needed to, mostly to avoid pissing off and letting down my parents—with an occasional ditch day once in a blue moon.

I hated school because I saw everyone around me including my own parents struggling just to survive and provide for their families, always stressed, and always worried about money. I figured if that's the reward that awaits me in my adult life for my long hours of studying and all around stress, then fuck it, why bother?

I had led a life of petty crime like shoplifting and auto burglary until that day I proposed we hit a bank.

So Ned and I discussed who would go in the bank and eventually settled on me since it was my idea. I grabbed a blank sheet of white paper from a nearby shelf and proceeded to cut it down to the size of a check. I continued by putting on a pair of black baseball (now burglary) gloves I had for obvious reasons and removed any possible prints off the paper by wiping it down with a cloth.

Next I grabbed a pen and wrote "SMILE" in chicken scratch (to avoid handwriting analysis) at the top center of my blank-check-sized paper.

Below it I wrote, "Put the money on the counter. No ink packs, alarms, or tracing devices. There's two more guys outside with guns, hurry up, this ain't no joke," also in chicken scratch. I emptied the contents of my wallet and removed any possible fingerprints from it as well. Then placed my new demand note inside the bill area of the wallet. I did this so when I approached the counter it would appear to everyone around me that I was simply attempting to cash a check.

We already had a vehicle outside just itching to be used as a getaway car, so now I simply needed a disguise.

I settled on the bank robbers' time-honored tradition of a hat and sunglasses—fucking flawless. We then discussed what bank we should hit. Through the teachings of *The FBI Files*, I knew we wanted to hit one near a residential area that was also somewhat close to a freeway. Most suspects on the show would head straight to the freeway after their heist, and the cops would usually be waiting.

I suggested that a second "legit" car of a totally different appearance than our stolen one should wait for us a few blocks away from our target and in a residential area. That way we could switch cars leaving the stolen one and its vehicle description behind. Then do the speed limit all the way home as I ducked down in back. We recruited another friend to help drive the second car.

We gave a friend I'll refer to as Bob a call notifying him of an opportunity in the here and now and informed him if he wanted in, to swing on by, like yesterday! Less than fifteen minutes later, Bob was there.

Ned and I presented Bob with the plan. He responded the only way I knew he would: "Hell yeah, I've always wanted to rob a bank."

This was perfect. I'd be getting paid and making my friend's dream come true.

Bob was a large, dark-skinned *cholo* (Hispanic gang member) and came dressed as such with the typical shaved head, oversized flannel shirt with deep, ironed creases up the sleeves, baggy oversized jeans, also with creases front and back, and a pair of Lugs. I was right there stylin' with him on the apparel, but we'd have to work past it and just keep it cool on the way to our mark. As long as we didn't attract attention to ourselves, we'd be all right.

I suggested we hit a bank on East H Street and Otay Lakes Road, which is located in the city of Bonita. We were all familiar with the streets there, and I knew we had a good chance of shaking any cops if need be. It was one of those small branches located inside a grocery store, but the location itself was good.

We would be able to pull out of the driveway after the robbery and take a right onto East H. Then we could drive down a few blocks, pull into the residential area where our legit car was waiting on us, and smoothly make our transition to our second vehicle. We went over it a few times, pumped ourselves up with talk of the insane money that awaited us, said fuck it, and headed out.

Ned and I headed to the stolen car while Bob headed to his own. Anytime in the past that we stole a car, a legit ride would follow directly behind us on streets and freeways. If a cop pulled up behind the legit car, the driver would intentionally swerve to entice the officer into pulling him over, letting the stolen car get away clean.

Now that wasn't something I saw on TV. It was our idea to put a legit car behind just in case the guys in the stolen vehicle had to get out and run. The legit could then come along and scoop them up. But only homies who were not on probation or parole could drive the legit car and risk getting stopped, and by even the ninth grade, most of my friends were not willing to take the risk going back to juvie or boys camp. I was the clean one and often drove the legit car.

We followed our procedure all the way to Bonita. Once there both cars pulled into the residential area, so we could see exactly where to go after the caper. All three of us had cell phones and could easily keep a line of communication open. It was time to rock and roll. We left the residential area and headed to the bank.

I was nervous as hell, but the plan was already in motion. We pulled into the shopping plaza and parked in a row of spaces near the front door of our intended target. The car was reversed into the spot for a quick getaway if needed. I looked at my partner and said, "Fuck it, let's do it!"

Once I left the vehicle, my eyes were fixed to the front entrance, and then I realized I forgot the fucking bag for the money at the pad. I looked back in the car for anything I could find and grabbed a paper takeout bag from Carl's Junior that had been on the floor. I tucked the bag in my pocket and began my walk to the store entrance at a steady pace—all the while losing my shit inside my own head.

Ned waited behind the wheel with the engine running, vigorously keeping point for any signs of trouble while he listened to his oldies. Part of his job description was to call me immediately if he spotted anything funny. I could then make my escape through the emergency back-door exit and get swooped up by the legit car a few blocks and backyards down.

I continued my nervous walk and entered the store, passing people as they left with their groceries. I looked to my left where the three bank teller stations were set up and took notice of the long line of customers waiting patiently to handle their banking needs. I wasn't sure what the right move was, so I just stood in line behind about six other people and waited for my turn.

And waited. I was wearing oversized, creased Solo jeans, a button-up short-sleeved flannel, black sunglasses, gloves, and a white-and-black hat. It was hot that day, I remember that. I tried keeping my hands in my pockets to conceal the fact I was wearing gloves inside on a hot-ass day like a crazy person, but it didn't really work that well.

Patrons and employees looked my way on several different occasions. I stood out, badly. Seems being dressed like a bank-robbing cholo while in line at a bank was somewhat suspicious.

I questioned myself and the plan at this point. It seemed like a complete bust, but now I was next in line. My nerves were kicking in majorly. I looked around several times to make sure no one was creeping up on me, and then I heard it, a young woman's cheery voice said, "Next."

One more quick thought: Walk out and say it was a bust or just fucking do it? If I don't do it, the homies will think I'm a bitch, I thought to myself. Can't be having that. I looked at the young and very attractive woman, then casually walked up to her counter.

She had noticed me standing in line looking like the poster child for bank robbery, but just smiled as I steadily approached her. Once at the counter I said something to the effect of, "Hello, how are you?" to my new customer service agent. I reached for my wallet, removing it from my back pocket.

She replied with the usual, "Fine, and yourself?" in a soft, sexy voice. I said nothing and continued by opening up my wallet. I then removed the note that rested in the billfold.

I set the note down on the counter and slid it across closer to her. At this point she appeared to know exactly what was happening, even without having yet read the note. The note was slightly bent from having been inside my wallet with me sitting on it, sweating the whole way there. She separated the bend with the index and middle finger of her right hand and began to read.

I literally forgot I had written "SMILE" at the top of the note, and when she did in fact smile at me, it seemed genuine and a little flirty. I realized I was completely wrong, but she was hot and I was nervous. For a brief moment I actually pondered asking for her number since she appeared to be into bank robbers, but ultimately decided against it for the conflict of interest.

After reading the note, she asked, "Do you have a bag, or do you need one?" Now that's the kind of fucking customer service I'm talking about right there. Friendly and helpful.

I replied, "No, I have one," and pulled the crinkled burger bag from my pocket. She opened the drawer and began to place the money on the counter. I grabbed the stacks of money as they hit the counter, bending them first to feel for any ink packs (thanks, *FBI Files*) and placed them in my paper bag.

Once the drawer was emptied, I grabbed my note, said thank you, turned, and walked toward the front entrance. It seemed everyone was staring at that point. About halfway to the doors, my nerves got the best of me, and I took off running toward the car faster than you can say, "*Yo quiero*, Taco Bell."

I hopped in and yelled, "GO FOOL, FUCKIN' GO!" with my heart racing inside my chest. Ned casually pulled out of the space using his fucking turn signal, oldies still playing, and asked, "What took so long?"

"There was a line, let's get the fuck out of here, fool!"

Ned continued driving at a steady pace passing the entrance doors I had just zoomed out of. We finally reached the driveway and made a righthand turn onto East H Street.

"Let me see the money," my chauffeur demanded. I reached into the bag grabbing as much as I could with one hand, pulling out nothing but hundreds and fifties with a couple of stale fries hanging out of the clump of cash.

We both stared at the loot for a second, marveling at its glory. I put the cash back in the bag and placed it on my lap, turned to Ned and asked, "When we gonna do this shit again, fool?" with a smile on my face.

He quickly said, "Shit, you tell me!"

As we drove down East H Street, three police cruisers flew by going the opposite direction in more than a hurry. My friend stayed cool and drove at a steady pace. I commenced to sift through the contents of the bag, looking for any tracing devices. None were present. I then ripped the paper bands off the money and threw the bank-stamped evidence out the window.

We pulled into the residential area where our legit car was stationed and swapped rides, locking up our stolen car behind us (there was a high rate of car theft in the area at the time). I lay down on the backseat as low as I possibly could, praying to god we didn't get pulled over on the way home. Luckily we didn't.

That was it. I had robbed my first bank for a Taco Bell grande combo meal. In all the world I was the fattest skinny person I knew of. What kind of shit is that?

2

ON MY BLOCK

I DIDN'T START out being a bank robber. I knew the rules of the street. This isn't a "poor me" story or "if I can be successful, you can too" or "gang kid goes to prison, comes out a changed man and makes good." No, this is my story about the neighborhood struggle I lived with each and every day on the mean streets in Southern California and how the neighborhood struggle eventually led me down a path I saw clearly in front of me. Was I a victim? Nah. That's how it was.

You see, at Castle Park Middle School in 1995 and 1996, the rules to survive middle school were obvious by the end of the first day. Don't dress or talk like a square, and be ready to fight whenever needed.

Grade school had been an entirely different ball game than what awaited me in middle and high school. Kids can be dicks. My family didn't have much money. So naturally 90 percent of my clothes came from thrift stores—basically from various senior citizens' closets.

When I hit middle school, other kids took notice of my apparel and how it did not line up with their own more trendy shit. It's not easy being eleven years old and dressing like a retiree in a senior living community out on the prowl for a date—plus off-brand white tennis shoes. I know this from experience. This creates a stressful problem for a child my age who was not looking to be considered an outsider.

I was constantly asked by other kids at school (in childish, condescending ways) why I would wear the same clothes so often, why we had an old beat-up Buick, why my shoes were falling apart, and why I never had money to go to the school store for extra snacks.

This shit wasn't gonna fly with me. I wasn't a violent kid, and I had the sense to know I couldn't fight everyone who threw a hurtful comment my way. Nevertheless, I may have fought a few that took it too far. I didn't like the fact that these pretentious little assholes were clowning me simply because their families seemed to have more money than mine. I wanted desperately to fit in and not be the poorest looking kid.

In the lunch area, a school store sold soda, candy, chips, nachos, and various other snacks. Each teacher had a stack of Pepsi coupons readily available in their desk. These coupons were given out to students for reasons mostly associated with some sort of small academic accomplishment or good test score. The cards would allow a student one free large soda at the school store.

The school also had a free lunch program for those who qualified. I did not qualify as my parents made just enough money to put us over that fine line. The free lunch program was a calendar sticker that the school administrators would place on the back of a student's ID each month. This would allow the student to show the lunch server that he or she is a member of this program, and the lunch worker would initial off on the date, to avoid double-ups.

My time to shine was toward the end of lunch when they'd give away any excess food at the Pizza Hut or Taco Bell stations. Nothing beat an extra bean and cheese burrito, so we hungry, growing boys got back in line for the handouts.

One afternoon during lunch, a friend and I decided to throw an M-80 firecracker that I had acquired on a trip to my grandmother's house in Tijuana. We lit it and threw it into the girls' restroom, which was directly in front of the school lunch area. We knew for a fact that shit would be hilarious, and it was indeed.

We did not, however, take into account how fucking loud it would actually be. It sounded like a small bomb had exploded echoing off the tiled walls.

Girls came running out, the lunch crowd stopped and looked, teachers came sprinting to the scene. No one was hurt, so the joke was a success. Of course a fellow unknown student later dimed me out.

I believe my sentence was three days of suspension and two weeks after-school detention for that particular incident. At detention I was assigned to help the school custodian for one hour after school cleaning the classrooms and offices.

You see, the custodian would open up a row of classrooms for me. He would then move on to the next row while I finished up cleaning those. I had free reign over several teachers' offices and their desk drawers. While sifting through each teacher's desk, I would remove a few Pepsi coupons and maybe some nice pens and random knickknacks.

I want to say a large soda at the school store was $1.25 at the time. I had zero problems getting rid of those Pepsi coupons for fifty cents a pop. My friends were as likely to see a teacher give them a Pepsi coupon as I was, so they were impressed to see I had stacks of 'em.

I played it cool and would only take three or four from each classroom at a time, depending on the available amount. I had also come across several stacks of sheets in an administrative office that contained the lunch cards. Those would get me at least five bucks a pop. So I shoved the stack in my waistband and took them all.

My foray into petty theft in middle school was nothing new. I'd had practice. In third grade I once had a hustle going where I'd steal some *Playboys* while walking to school. I'd stop in at this little liquor store and snake a few each week on the walk in.

I was white, and in third grade, so the shop owner suspected nothing. Suckers. I'd slang the *Playboys* at school for five bucks each to the fifth and sixth graders. Those motherfuckers had good money. That only lasted as long as it took for the owner to notice his inventory was off, I guess.

Off of this little hustle in the teachers' desks in middle school, I was able to buy some new, more stylish clothes and snack as much as I damn well pleased from the school store in just a few days. That shit felt damn good. Plus it seemed like my small wad of cash, combined with my abundance of nachos and large sodas, was attracting the ladies my way. Stealing was going to be my golden ticket.

Soon I was making suspension a regular thing just so I could hang back after school and get paid.

One of my favorite suspensions came about because of a half ounce of liquid latex I deliberately applied to the leg hairs of one of my enemies. The liquid in the bottle solidified into a gummy substance, like when you're trying to get glue off your hands by rubbing them together, and you get that build up. It dries like that.

I had a couple extra bottles of it left over from a previous Halloween and had been wondering what to do with them. So one day in class I doused this dude's above-average hairy-ass leg with a bottle's worth.

I got anything his shorts weren't covering on the left side of his shin and calf. Don't expect an explanation of why he was an enemy by the way, he just was. So he tells on me. Actually that pretty much sums up why I didn't like him right there. Constantly tattling. One shaved leg of my enemy later and I'm suspended with a one-week detention. Hell yeah! I know it was a dick move now, by the way, but at the time, his regular snitchery was unforgivable.

In a couple months the Pepsi coupon well started to dry up, along with the lunch card money. Apparently the teachers had taken notice that their supply of coupons was often running low, and they began to lock them up.

Lucky for me, walking to and from school each day afforded me the opportunity to pass by many stores along the way, or through short alternate routes. The solution to my dry well was obvious: steal some other shit and sell it. I didn't have the courage to try it on my own, so I asked a friend to partner up with me in my new venture. Lucky for me there was no problem finding a friend to help. Actually the first one I asked agreed.

Kevin had been my dumpster-diving partner as a child. We would hit a dumpster behind the Lucky's grocery store on Orange and Melrose. The workers would toss fruit snacks and pastries on the day of their expiration. We'd climb on in and fill up bags with some bomb shit.

Once we had our bounty, we'd climb our way up a ladder mounted on the side of the grocery chain's building, pick a spot on the roof with no syringes, sit down and proceed to grub. That shit may have been expired, and may have come from a trash can, but it was still in boxes, and it was good shit at the time.

Most of my friends and associates were other young, financially lacking individuals with an equal or greater amount of free time as I had. My business associate/friend and I discussed our plan during lunch and agreed to hit the Target store over on Palomar and Broadway.

We'd go in with no real target in mind and take anything of value we knew could get us something at school. We would then share in the spoils 50/50 as long as we both walked out with DVDs, electric shavers, or video games, stuff like that. Equal risks deserved equal rewards. We mostly stuck to sifting through the return carts parked for restocking in the aisles (as the theft magnets had already been deactivated), and our plan worked flawlessly for most of middle school. DVDs could bring $5 and video games $10.

I realized I wasn't doing anything big-time, but, man, it felt good to just have new clothes from the mall, not Goodwill, and to also fit in with everyone else just a little. I'd sometimes go to the grocery store and snatch up some food for the house when I was in middle school.

My mom's gonna lose her shit when she reads this part, but I've had more Tombstone pizzas and packs of bacon shoved down the front of my pants than I'd care to admit. I'd swipe them from the Lucky's and then take the food home and place it in the freezer for the family to enjoy.

I like Tombstone pizzas and love bacon. Way I saw it, I was just doing my part for the household. Other times I'd walk to nearby farmers markets and do carne asada runs where I'd put in an order for a couple pounds at the meat section, then just run out the door. I'd get it back home and put it in the fridge. But only when I saw things were rougher than usual, that is. Sorry, Mom.

You're probably picturing me as a young, overweight Mexican kid because I talk about food so much. In truth, I was taller than most, as white as cocaine, thin, with a noticeable varrio accent and brown, slicked-back hair. Most of the homies in the neighborhood back then were of average height and build, Hispanic, with shaved heads or black hair. So I stood out as much as a random red tortilla chip. Not a desired attribute in the hood.

My mother is white and birth father too, but the man I call father is Hispanic. He married my mother, raised me, and paid the bills, so it would be disrespectful not to recognize him as my father.

Now about that varrio accent. *Varrio* means neighborhood or barrio in Spanish. That was my neighborhood, my hood. My homies were Hispanic and spoke Spanish. It was rare that someone would grow up there not speaking Spanish. I speak Spanish too and have the accent because that's how we sounded down there. Just due to our region I guess.

I dressed cholo in baggy, too-big clothing with deeply ironed creases in my shirts and super-baggy jeans. We'd get extra-large-sized jeans with added bagginess at the bottom. That was to fit over the tongue of our shoes, well, to fall just enough so only about two rows of shoelaces were exposed. Sometimes I'd cut the whole bottom off the pants, make a one-inch slit in the sides and cuff 'em up with a little fold. Some homies stapled their pant cuffs, but I used rubber cement and ironed it tight.

I began to get more creative with my thefts over time. Soon I was hitting Miller's Outpost (a store at the Chula Vista mall). I would go dressed in Dickie shorts and a short-sleeve flannel that was only fastened at the top three buttons, exposing my tucked-in undershirt just a bit. I would grab three or four pairs of jeans and take them to the dressing room.

I'd remove the security tag from my desired pair of pants. Then remove both my shirts and unbutton my shorts. I'd wrap the tag-free pair of $50 jeans around my torso and secure them there with car bungie cords with hooks on the end, which had been tucked in my pockets.

I would then put on my shirts, tucking the undershirt back in and secure my waistband to fit over as much of the pants as possible. The loose security tag would be wedged underneath the fitting room chair, and the top three buttons of my flannel would be refastened. I would finish by returning the other jeans to their shelves and casually walking out. I used the same process for shirts and would stay geared up (looking sharp).

So basically, stealing was my escape and my reward. Yes, I'd have to put up with daily bullshit that comes with living in the hood and, yes, possibly dodge some security guards or cops, but I'd be living through it all a little more comfortably in between.

Like walking to school, I always carried a weapon, usually a knife. If cops didn't stop me, then it would be a carload of who knows who. I learned that as long as I didn't run, they wouldn't feel empowered. In fact, I'd reach behind my back and approach a mystery car filled with four or five guys I didn't know. Yah, I could have gotten shot, but at least I'd know what was coming.

You could drive five minutes east of where I grew up in San Diego and be in a completely different place—and another five minutes more and you'd be in swanky neighborhoods with multimillion-dollar homes. I knew things were better elsewhere. I just wanted to do everything I could to get over there.

3

IF YOU GET KNOCKED DOWN, YOU COME BACK STRONGER

VARRIO OTAY, RLS (Rasta Locos), Otay RBLS (River Bottom Locos), Otay 13, VLSO (Vatos Locos Otay), Otay Zone, 1513—gang tags were followed by a list of names.

On my walk to school, I used to enjoy looking at the names written in graffiti on all the street posts, mailboxes, curbs, windows, and walls of my neighborhood and picture them as individuals and wonder how these guys got their names. These signs were constant reminders and caution signs written in various colors of spray-paint on damn near any available surface—notifying you of exactly where you were.

I liked some names more than others. I remember seeing a lot of the seven dwarf names written in graffiti next to any variation of Otay, but I never saw Bashful up there. I remember joking with a friend that poor ol' Bashful must not have made the cut, or the other six dwarfs had a grudge and took him out.

Otay Zone was always my favorite. I just liked the way it sounded. The gang itself was believed to have originally been founded in the 1920s or 1930s. Otay is the gang name. The other labels are names of the cliques, such as Otay River Bottom, a separate group, whose name just depends on the region of the neighborhood you're from.

Otay itself was a small, but proud neighborhood. A lot of the parents and grandparents of my fellow students had originally started off as immigrants, including my own dad who later gained legal residency, but I still have his family in Mexico. I didn't have any other family living in San Diego except for an eighty-something great aunt up in El Cajon. So I had no cousins or older brothers to fall back on if I had any issues.

People in my community were hard-ass workers and appreciated everything they achieved through the chances they were provided. Off of Albany and Main there's Otay Park. The community often came together there to barbecue or throw small parties for kids.

Toward the back of the small park was an even smaller green hill that ended at someone's property line. That line was marked by a white fence.

The homies many years prior had put an Old English "OTAY" in roughly five-foot letters at the center of this fence in black spray-paint, always watching over the park. Due to recent renovations, the white fence is now a cinder-block wall, but the spray-painted *OTAY* still remains—a graffiti'd embodiment of neighborhood pride. A few different artists and their styles have put it up over the years, but nothing in the hood beat the view of those classic 1990s Old English letters across that white fence.

The park once had a wooden sign at the front that read OTAY PARK to welcome newcomers. You could regularly find the homies at the benches there posted at odd hours of the night, keeping watch for any enemies with ill intent. I'm guessing during the homies' shift change or something, a rival gang chopped that sign down with an ax, clear down at the base of both its posts. Two little hacked wooden post stumps greeted any newcomers to our park for quite a while.

I always appreciated the fact that a rival gang chopped the sign down instead of one of us. They can still suck a dick though. Now the sign's a little more sturdy and made of concrete.

Otay Park with the Old English lettering. My hood.

That's how it is if you're raised in Otay. If you get knocked down, you come back stronger.

After school the older high school kids would congregate across the street from the front of our middle school entrance to the tune of about twenty to thirty boys and girls. If you can picture any stereotypical cholo or chola from a movie, you're on the right track.

Just picture them as thirteen- to fifteen-year-olds, and now you're all the way there: creased-up Ben Davis pants over Nike Cortez or Adidas, black Dickie belt hanging low, Locs (the preferred type of sunglasses popularized by Eazy E), with a creased-up shirt. Pretty much like the characters from the film *187*, but a little younger, and Samuel L. Jackson wasn't a teacher there.

Fights were common. Always. Before, during, and after school. The favorite spot to handle business for the entire community it seemed was the Loma Verde Park located down First Avenue from Quintard Street. I found myself attending an after-school fight at said park. My close friend/shoplifting partner Kevin had invited me.

Turned out it wasn't so much a fight, but an attack. It may have been spontaneous for all I know, but the rumbly mob of troubled youths all seemed to get equally agitated as two people neared the park.

This was obviously information that wasn't relayed to one of the parties involved, because the motherfucker came with no backup but a single friend. So I'm assuming it was originally scheduled for a one-on-one match. The gatherings for fights at this particular park would have regular turnouts of about sixty to eighty people after school, as the high school was just as close to the park as our own middle school was.

Younger adult gang members already knew it was the spot for entertainment after school hours. So they'd regularly be there, posted on the park benches, along with some high school–aged gangsters just chilling and enjoying the fights.

So on this day it wasn't anything new to see a large turnout and for a big chunk of that turnout to be gang members. No real red flags went off until this guy and his friend set foot on that park grass. This fucking kid and his friend got pounced on and beat like they stole something by about twenty different gangsters of various ages.

Turned out he had just pissed off the wrong person's little cousin. For what, I don't know. After a while I realized they appeared to be getting bored of beating these kids into ketchup. But the crowds cheered on. A few of the homies that had participated rested and talked near a white metal park sign near the entrance of the park. The sign looked like it may have once been a reflective white surface. It now had Otay Zone written in blue spray-paint, across a weather-beaten, semi-reflective, off-white background.

I suggested to Kevin that we dip out (leave). I knew I stood out and I knew I didn't want to get smashed on (beaten up) by various generations of gangsters for any reason. Kevin told me not to trip (don't overreact, and chill out) and pointed to one of the gangsters that had remained seated drinking his beer at the park bench.

"That's my cousin, he's cool! Let's go over and say what's up to him real quick."

I agreed and found myself walking with Kevin straight into uncertainty. Will I be well received? Will I be the new focus of attention for the mob?

I was glad to not be one of those guys on the ground, but I wanted to keep it that way. So I remained cautious. We made our way over to the roughly eighteen-year-old cousin of my friend. He was geared up with oversized, black creased Ben Davis jeans, a button-up short-sleeved gray and white flannel, white Nike Cortez, and for the finishing touch, a pair of Locs. He was at the arena with a chick that oddly enough fit his exact clothing description, except she had a flannel over a tube top.

As we were walking his direction, I observed some of the currently winded gangsters taking notice of us, and our curious path. They must have recognized Kevin as being a relative of someone, because we didn't get one level of disrespect or resistance along the way to the bench.

At the bench Kevin walked up to his cholo'd out older cousin, let's call him Steve, and lightly slapped his hand, which was then followed by a fist bump and simply, "What's up?" with an upward nod of his head.

Kevin then introduced me to his cousin. I followed the introduction procedure I had just witnessed flawlessly, and said, "Hey what's up, man, I'm Richard." I fucken nailed it.

Steve then responded with, "*Orale mucho gusto.* Steve, Otay," which identified cousin Steve as a full-fledged member of the same gang that controlled the streets I walk on every day to and from school. He was also from the same gang as the pack of bloody-shoed gang members that stood just feet away. The next words ol' Steve said caught me off guard entirely.

He looked at me, with a couple seconds passing, and then hit me with, "Where the fuck you from?"

I definitely wasn't ready for that. So as I wrapped my head around what I had just been asked, somewhat confused about the question itself, and as to why Steve would be interested in my birthplace or upbringing, I uttered, "I live behind the market on

Orange and Hilltop," while pointing in the general direction of my apartment complex.

Judging by the laughter from Kevin and his cousin, I knew I had messed that one up.

Kevin, while looking at me, still laughing a little, chimed in, and a little late may I add, said, "He means what neighborhood are you from?"

Now I'm just fucking perplexed. I'd never been asked this before up until that point, so I responded with the only correct answer I thought there was: "I'm from right here."

Steve responded, "That's right, lil' homie!" and quickly got sidetracked by something Kevin had asked him. I promptly said my goodbyes, excused myself, told Kevin I'd see him later, and got the fuck up outta there.

Prior to this I had had no direct conversations with any members of Otay. Only their family members I went to school with. Kids would often brag about how their older brother, cousins, parents, or even grandparents were from Otay. After seeing what happened to those two kids at the park, I knew I needed to start expanding my friendship circle. I figured some connections to more homies from Otay could most definitely be beneficial.

The gangsters in my neighborhood were looked at as untouchable, god-like figures to us kids. We would constantly hear the stories of money, girls, parties, and respect from the younger family members of the gangsters at school. No one fucked with a member, or their families. Some of my friends were basically present for most of the at-home gangster gatherings simply because, well, they slept in the next room. We would see the homies ourselves every day with new pressed clothes and with fine-ass girls by their side.

It seemed like a pretty good life to me, but I wasn't necessarily seeking that exact lifestyle. I didn't have any friends from Otay, and I had been able to get by so far without them. Why make it a thing now? I already had to worry about getting shot or stabbed enough as it was. So I just kept doing me, and only had occasional circumstantial encounters with members of Otay for a while.

Even with that being the case, I still had another group of feared individuals to dodge every day outside of school: the Chula Vista police department. Let me tell you about these motherfuckers for a minute, and keep in mind that I'm speaking on the officers between let's say 1994 and 2001.

These fucking guys had me up against cars, patted down, in cuffs, sitting on a curb, and accused of being a gang member, in that order usually, since I was in the fifth or sixth grade. Shit, law enforcement told me I was from Otay long before any homies did.

Police harassment wasn't my biggest concern, as inconvenient as being detained for twenty minutes to an hour and put on display in cuffs for all passersby to gawk at was. It wasn't anything compared to what would happen if the Chula Vista police decided you were on their shit list. For someone to find their way onto said shit list took very little, sometimes nothing at all. One could simply be related to a parolee that the cops are not too fond of, talk back to an officer when you were upset about being placed in cuffs for no apparent reason, all while they desperately looked for a reason to take you in—any reason.

My personal favorite was denying you were a gang member. They did not like that one bit. To be accused of being a gang member by the wrong officer went something like this: You're walking down the street in your neighborhood at any given time of day. A cop pulls up behind you rapidly, gets out of his patrol car, and yells for you to stop where you are. Then it's up against the car, pat down, cuffs, sit on the curb, and let the accusations and insults begin.

Questions by the CVPD during those years for walking or driving down the street were typically as follows:

OFFICER: You on probation or parole?

ME: No.

OFFICER: [Depending on age, they'd follow it up with...] You got any warrants? You ever been arrested?

ME: No.

Officer begins to get irritated at my lack of a criminal record by this point.

IRRITATED Officer: Where you coming from?

ME: The store.

IRRITATED Officer: Where you headed to?

ME: Home.

OFFICER: Where do you live?

ME: [I give my address.]

Officer starts talking into his radio, desperately hoping I have something, fucking anything at all that'll get me on my way to juvie.

OFFICER: How long you been from Otay?

Here's where the fun would start.

ME: I'm not.

OFFICER: [laughing] Don't fucking lie to me, kid, look how you're dressed.

ME: I'm not lying.

If that was my first interaction with this particular officer, I might get cut loose soon after with a warning, yes, a warning for fucking walking. You rarely see an officer only once in a lifetime, though, when you live in their patrol area. So it was this second encounter that would usually end the line of questioning like this:

OFFICER: How long you been from Otay?

ME: I'm not.

Officer laughs.

OFFICER: Then you won't mind if I drop you off over on Woodlawn and J street right?

ME: But I live right down the street from here.

OFFICER: That's not what I asked you.

ME: I'll just walk home from here.

OFFICER: Okay, so you are from Otay?

ME: No, I just don't want to take the bus and walk for no reason.

OFFICER: You need to stop lying or I'm gonna charge you with providing false information to a police officer!

ME: I'm not from Otay.

OFFICER: Okay, let's go.

And off we'd go.

Now for those of you unfamiliar with the Chula Vista area, you might be saying to yourself, well what's so bad about Woodlawn and J? Well I'll tell you what's wrong with it. It's the heart of one of Otay's biggest rival neighborhoods.

Now as a young kid, I didn't have much to worry about in terms of being from a gang, or most of the problems and stress that go with it; however, you could still find yourself in a bad spot with the local gangsters of that area regardless.

All it took was for someone on the street to not recognize me as a local and I could be in for some serious shit. Luckily cell phones weren't a big thing back then, or at least us hood folk couldn't afford them in the midnineties. So calling reinforcements wasn't really an option. If one gangster saw you, you'd only have to deal with one gangster. Unless he had homies nearby within an ear shot of a distress whistle.

Now I'm not saying this happened every time I had a run-in with an officer, but when I would, it would suck, plain and simple. It was only about a five-mile walk back home from there, but I would not make that walk in a comfortable state of mind. Best case, I dodge a couple gangsters, have a long walk, and get yelled at by my parents later for disappearing and not telling anyone. Worst case, well, I die, I guess.

You may be asking yourself at this point, why didn't I tell my parents what was going on? Well because a free ride from the cops wasn't the worst they'd do for you. I'm not gonna fake the funk and say I was beaten by these officers or anything, because I wasn't. Others weren't so fortunate, though, and many homies caught an ass beating courtesy of the CVPD often.

You see, the favorite technique for a Chula Vista police officer at the time to get results was to find a mystery bag of drugs on you or your property, wallet, or car and then proceed to ask you questions regarding the gang or your knowledge of any particular crimes they were currently investigating. I saw it happen to Boomer from Otay firsthand.

You may be saying, yeah fucking right, I see those dumb-ass excuses on the show *Cops* all the time. Well you'd be absolutely right to have that opinion; it is a dumb-ass excuse. Believe me, they realize this.

Public perception is that our police officers can do no wrong. Who's gonna believe some broke-ass neighborhood kid over an officer of the law? Usually no one does. All cops aren't bad, but they're definitely all human, and human beings do fucked-up shit from time to time.

Sometimes the cops would let you go if they actually believed you had no knowledge of the issues you were presented with. Sometimes they wouldn't. All for doing absolutely nothing wrong. That treatment was usually reserved for anyone they believed may have committed a crime at some point—and just hadn't been caught yet. But it could also be the officer's solution to a grudge.

Like this example: Let's say a homie spray-painted a gang name on a cop car—not even his own gang name, and he certainly didn't sign it. So the cops are now bringing the heat down on everybody, just people walking down the street because of whoever spray-painted shit on their car. Not that the cops would find out the perpetrator. This technique served to signal to the community to take care of the problem spray-painter themselves. Like the cops are saying, "You take care of this dude."

So, do I tell my mom and dad about the harassment and potentially get sent to juvie at any time with a drug record? Or keep quiet, start running from the police when I see them as a precautionary measure, and continue my normal program? I took option two.

I didn't want to bring any unnecessary attention to my home because my dad was going through the immigration process to become a citizen. I didn't want cops taking out any grudges on our family.

Here's the thing that bugs me most about this particular reflection. People hear these stories and sometimes find humor in them and then justify the possibility of the officer actually planting drugs on a suspect (child or adult) because, well obviously, the guy must have deserved it for whatever reason. Or the officers do what they have to in order to keep us safe from people like that! Okay cool, noted.

Now keep in mind that the officer most likely confiscated those drugs from a previous suspect that he then let go—more than likely after said suspect gave up his dealer.

The officer or officers then do not report the drugs, so they can then plant them on someone else later who ends up pissing them off. That means the officer let an actual, real-life verified offender go, then transported the drugs—unlawfully at that— to plant those drugs on another person and finished off with a false police report. That particular officer not only committed the same crime that he or she is now charging some other poor asshole with, but the officer literally committed the only crimes to take place at all.

Consider this: In the midnineties, if you had two previous strikes, a judge under law had to commit you to serve no less than twenty-five years to life for *any* new felony conviction, violent or not. Even if two of those strikes were acquired as a juvenile. And it all comes down to your word against theirs.

Before anyone attempts to justify that inhumane law, just wonder, would you be okay with your son or daughter being taken away for no less than a quarter century for stealing a bike from someone's lawn at night? Fucked up thought, huh?

This is the system I grew up in, and those are the people I'm supposed to listen to and trust as a child? To count on? To turn to?

From that point on, whenever I heard, "Stop where you are" or "Stop or I'll shoot" (usually that's said when they're already chasing you down), and I was on foot near some fences, I'd make a break for it. If you're now thinking that seems a little extreme, that some police officers are cool, why run from them all? Well, reader, it's because at that age I hadn't yet had the pleasure of meeting a cool cop in my many encounters, that's why.

Slowly but surely some of my peers began to join the gang throughout middle school. By eighth grade I had around seven classmates and friends who were full members. Every single one of them had older family members from the hood. Pressure would then be put on the other friends by the freshly knighted gangsters to also join.

My game was making money through shoplifting from stores and maybe taking a few things out of a parked car, and I didn't see the potential for focusing on that being from a gang. Most homies were related to someone else from the neighborhood. So not being constantly surrounded with that life at home helped sway my reluctance I'm sure. But not for long.

4
REFUSE TO LOSE

RACE WAS A small factor in middle school with only a few rumbles between the Hispanic and African American students happening in both my years there. I can only recall one racial altercation at middle school actually happening on school grounds at lunch break back by a group of tables near the PE area.

High school was much different. Skin tone mattered.

During my first day at Castle Park High, my fourteen-year-old self was greeted by the school's principal, Mr. Winter, the minute I walked onto campus.

We called him "The Winter Man." He was thin and stood about 6 feet 6 and knew exactly who I was and exactly how many times I had been suspended at my previous school down the street. I'm guessing he was given a list of students to watch out for.

I ended up not caring too much for this particular principal as he made it a habit to photograph students' binders that contained graffiti with the hopes of helping the local CVPD document some new gang members. Maybe he had good intentions, maybe not. I just know he got it wrong a couple of times. He advised me that my previous line of behavior in middle school would not be tolerated at Castle Park High. I heard what he had to say and then made my way wherever it was I needed to go.

At first break I really noticed the difference between high school and middle school. Large groups of students had voluntarily separated themselves by race. Mostly Hispanics in the majority, but blacks, and a handful of Asians (we'd battle to sit by them and copy off their tests because they were known to be smart). As a white guy, I didn't choose to segregate myself, but just up to that point I identified with the Hispanic group and also had white friends.

Only a few smaller groups were multiracial with the exception of the jocks who had a fairly large but diverse group. I linked up with several of my friends I had attended grade school and middle school with. Some were gang members by now, some not. We found our way over to where we'd hang out during all breaks in the year to come. We called it The Wall.

The homies before us had decided to set up shop against the outside of the art teacher's class, since who knows how many years before us. Part of the real estate package that came with The Wall were something like five or six round stone tables that sat directly outside in front of the art class. If you were an outsider, and you crossed those tables, it was all bad for you.

That first day, I was invited by my old dumpster-diving friend Kevin who now attended school with me to join him for some pizza and arcade games across the street at Liberty's Giant Pizza for lunch. Well shit, I'm fond of both pizza and games. I figured it's my first day and no teachers should miss me if I were to be late upon returning, so I agreed. I already knew this to be a popular hangout for our local gangsters, but figured I'd be fine since I was with Kevin and he had relatives from the hood.

We made our way toward the football field, which was located at the side of our campus. To avoid a much longer journey to Liberty's, we needed to escape the school grounds by crossing the football field and walking down a small, concrete staircase. After this point our only concern would be cops. Liberty's is maybe 300 feet from the bottom of that staircase. So if we made it that far, we were pretty much home-free, as long as there were no police parked near the back loading areas of the various stores of the plaza where Liberty's is located.

We reached the football field, took a few looks around for any teachers or administrators, and made our way across the large patch of grass. Now we didn't want to run across and garner any unneeded attention, so we just casually walked as though our mission were completely condoned.

About two thirds of the way through the field, as we continued to look around for any adults, Kevin noticed someone running our direction from the area we had originally departed from, and was quickly approaching the field in a full gallop.

Well fuck me sideways, if it wasn't The Winter Man himself. He was coming straight for us and quickly at that, with the intentions of ruining my lunch plans, no doubt. I notified Kevin by simply saying, "Oh shit, it's the principal!"

Call it force of habit or what you will, but I immediately took off running toward the staircase and determined midsprint that I would deal with any ramifications later, after I was home-free of course. I did not run for fun at that age, so if I were running, I'm not looking back.

I made it to the stairs and down in a flash. I ran toward some apartments directly behind the property Liberty's sits on and hid for a bit. After about ten minutes I came out and made my way to the pizza place hoping I'd find Kevin there. Nope. I later found out that Kevin's slow ass got caught. I scoped out Liberty's for any signs of police and stepped in the front entrance.

No Kevin, but as luck would have it, or at least my luck, there were around ten older teenaged gangsters eating pizza, playing arcade games, and just sitting around talking. I didn't recognize them. The best way I can describe what I felt at that moment would be that oh-shit feeling you get when you realize you fucked up.

I looked around and made my way to the sales counter, ordered a slice of pizza with a soda, then strolled to an available table, sat down, just hoped I didn't get the attention of some asshole looking for trouble, and waited for my pizza to be ready. No more than a minute into my wait, a roughly eighteen-year-old homie came my direction and noticeably tried to make eye contact.

He walked up to my table and asked, "Where you from, homie?"

By this time I had been hit up several times since my first experience in the park, which is what it means in the hood to ask another person what hood they're from, and knew exactly how to respond.

"I ain't from nowhere," I answered.

He then introduced himself. Let's call him Character. He said, "All right, homie, I'm Big Character from Otay River Bottom," and shook my hand with a light slap of the palm, followed by a fist bump.

The River Bottom is an area located near, well, a river. The Otay Valley River to be exact. It was a low-income housing project (I only say *was* because I don't know what rents are looking like these days), and everyone knew not to go down there without an invitation. A large chunk of Otay gang members lived there or lived near there and had decided to make it a clique of the gang many years prior.

I introduced myself by my first name and for some reason chose to ask if he knew cousin Steve. Not even really knowing the guy myself, I realized I may have fucked up, but I was trying to make small talk, I guess. He replied that he had seen him around the hood, but didn't know him too well.

A few moments of silence passed and then before my pizza could even find its way to the table, someone from outside and out of view shouted, "THE *JURAS!*" (the cops).

Everyone (including me) jumped up at once as a collective and began rushing to the back of the pizza shop and poured out of this small back entrance, dispersing in all directions.

At this point I didn't care if you were a gang member or a hyena in front of me, I'm getting by and getting gone. I just ran with all I had pushing my way past people who were only now realizing that buying yourself a pair of size 55 jeans for a skinny dude may not always be a good idea.

I made my way to a side entrance of the high school and snuck my way back onto campus. I was late but still waltzed up into class like nothing had happened, apologizing to the teacher for my tardiness and chalking it up to not knowing the layout of the school yet. She pointed out my seat and I settled right in, hating every moment of whatever class that was.

Nearing the end of class, any class, I would get anxious and impatient, as I seriously hated every class but two: art and some other shit. Don't ask me what the other was, I genuinely do not remember, only that it was tolerable because I had two friends in that class. I would just want to get the hell up out of there so I could meet up with the homies between classes to chop it up and shoot the shit before I headed to my next layer of hell.

Soon after I started high school, my parents bought our first house. A roughly 1,400-square-foot, four-bedroom, two-bath residence on the corner of Turquoise and Melrose. The property was surrounded by a waist-high chain link fence and had two large trees in the front yard and a smaller tree located on the Turquoise side of the house, but closer to the back. It had no grass in the front, just dirt, and nothing but weeds around three feet tall growing in the back.

The backyard was mostly a hill covered in ice plant, with only about a six-foot-wide strip of flat level ground at the base. Not pretty to look at, actually it was the most beat-up looking house on the block, but my parents finally did it, they got a house! We were all pretty excited about our new living situation. My level of excitement soon diminished after having a talk with my dad about improvements that could be made to the property.

You see my dad was raised in an extremely impoverished area of Tijuana. He and his younger brother built my grandma's house there from the ground up as children. The neighborhood had no running water or electricity, but it was their home that they built. My dad informed me of his new to-do list. Build a wrought-iron fence that would rest atop a cinder-block wall to take the place of our current fencing, build a wooden six-foot-tall fence along the property line on both the sides and back of the house, remove the back tree, and chop the hill in our backyard in half and then erect a cinder-block wall at the new base of the hill for support to create a more enjoyable backyard.

Those all sounded like awesome improvements, until I asked how much all that would cost. His response to my question was, "Not much, we'll just buy a couple pick axs, shovels, and whatever the material costs."

Oh fucking great, I thought to myself, this is gonna suck balls. I knew he wasn't joking—laziness and money to burn were not an option. There goes any free time I may have hoped for. So basically most of my "me" time was spent renovating the outside of the property for the next couple years and hustling when possible.

I wasn't an ungrateful child. I knew the least I could do was assist with the improvements that needed to be done. I loved my parents and wanted to do my part to make them happy. So skipping out on any work was not an option.

I played with my school schedule a little and squeezed in some extra time for myself. By this point I had acquired some new close friends whom we'll call Olaf, Roger, Hunter, and Boomer. Two were from Otay already, and the other two wanted to be, desperately. Four of us would eventually become members over the years. These would be the people I hung most tough with for the next few years. Hustling nonstop.

We spent most of our time planning out and then executing our shoplifting schemes and trying to pick up girls along our way. Hunter however thought we were thinking too small and wanted to expand our thefts to include cars. I always figured there was money in cars, but I had no idea how to steal one at the time. I also had no fucking clue what I'd do with a stolen car once I had it. I liked my shoplifting hustle just fine. Plus I lived at home with my parents. Can't really explain a Cobra in the driveway to Mom and Dad at fourteen years old.

5
LIL' HOMIES

My creative school schedule didn't work out as I had planned. By the end of the year I had successfully failed about every class except art. My parents were not thrilled, to say the least. My options at the time were to stay at Castle Park High and fall even further behind or go to an alternative school called The Learning Center to catch up a little quicker. I elected to give The Learning Center a shot for various reasons.

The alternative school was located on the same grounds as Castle Park High, but out near the parking lot tucked away in the corner. I would be given my work to take home for completion and be required to return it once every week during a two-hour class. Shit, that would be perfect for my schedule. Indeed. I was able to complete ten days of work in about two days, which gave me ample opportunity to carry out my shoplifting.

One day I decided to go with my old friend Kevin on a trip to Kmart. By this time we were taking preorders from other students who would give us a list of their desired but unaffordable items. We would then head to the needed stores to fill those orders and sell them at one third the value. A pretty good system I thought. That is until Kevin tried to steal around eight Fossil watches on this particular trip, greedy bastard. I gotta give it to him, he went biggish.

When we went to Kmart, our strategy was for one person to keep point, while the other loads up. Then make our exit through the gardening section. Flawless, we thought. We were only there for four watches total. I had already pocketed half the order and was keeping point for Kevin. I did my job just fine. From the other side of the watch stand while keeping look out, I noticed Kevin was taking much more time than was needed for two watches. Even though the coast was clear, I still didn't like it.

On our walk toward the gardening section, I asked Kevin what the hell took so long. He had apparently decided to capitalize on the fact that no one was around and load up with as many watches as possible. It sounded good in theory.

As we approached the gardening section at the end of the store, we noticed the exit doors were closed but not obviously locked, and we were being watched by staff. I knew exactly what was going on, as did Kevin. Butch and Sundance were surrounded.

Kevin obviously didn't know where my head was once I realized what we were walking into. The woman at the counter asked us to stop and wait there for a moment. Fuck that bitch and her red vest. I made a break for it!

I rushed the doors, pushing them open. Only to find a sheriff's deputy pulling up at that exact moment. I broke left and made my way around the back of the store and through some apartments behind it. No sign of Kevin or his slow-ass self, just me running with all I had and a deputy now in hot pursuit.

I've never heard "Stop or I'll shoot" as many times in my life to this day. I knew being caught was not an option for me. I would not only have to deal with an officer that more than likely would not be thrilled I made him run, but then also have to deal with my parents. No, thank you.

I began to get more of a lead on my new green shadow as I rushed through the apartment complex. I crossed a parking lot and beelined for a roughly six-foot-tall wooden fence. Without thinking, I grabbed the top of the fence and hurled my skinny self over.

Turns out the other side of the fence was an entirely different complex and had about a fifteen-foot drop that I was completely unaware of. I landed on a parking stop (that concrete block thing), hopped up, and continued my escape.

As I made my way through the new complex, I felt a considerable amount of pain in my back. My right leg was also acting up, which was preventing me from keeping up my running speed, but it seemed I had lost my green friend for now. I headed toward the front of the apartment complex, squeezed through a white iron gate, and realized I was on 4th Avenue and directly across the street from the Chula Vista Adult School.

Knowing the deputy wouldn't give up that easily, I hobbled my way across 4th in a hurry and entered the school property. Some students that were out front had clearly taken notice I was somewhat disheveled and limping, but didn't bother to question it. I navigated my way through the halls and found an open classroom door. I poked my head through the doorway, looking to see if I had a shot of blending in. I didn't see a teacher, but I didn't quite fit in either.

At fourteen, I was far younger than most of the twenty-somethings in this class. It would have to do. Once inside I removed a jacket I was wearing and readjusted my hair, trying to change my appearance as much as I could.

My plan worked fine. No teacher showed up for about an hour, and only a few students asked me who the hell I was and why I was there. I made my exit when the teacher returned to class, checked to make sure the coast was clear, and limped home.

No surprise. Kevin and his useless-ass legs got busted. He didn't get in much trouble since he hadn't exited the store with the property. He just had to deal with his mom and accept being banned from the store. He didn't mention my name during his temporary detention, as we all knew snitching was a no-go. Talking to Kevin about his ordeal and what he went through once I was gone revealed some useful information for future forays, as it turned out.

Kevin said Kmart's loss prevention officer notified him that he had in fact not seen Kevin put the watches in his pockets due to an obstructed view, but only that his hands were continuously going near his waistband. The loss prevention officer told him, "Anytime your hands go to your pockets, backpack, or waistband, we're on it." Good to know.

Kevin was discouraged by being caught and no longer wished to participate with any petty thefts in the future. His loss, the way I saw it. It's not my fault Kevin had the survival instincts of a Dodo bird and couldn't just fucking run.

What I took from that experience and the information I later obtained from Kevin was that if you don't put your hands in the red flag areas, then you're clearly not a person of interest. Now I just needed to figure out how I could steal merchandise without putting it in my pockets, backpack, or waistband. Challenge accepted.

After some time of thinking about my new mission, I remembered something I saw on TV recently where the thief had a hollow book with the pages carved out to create a storage area. Well shit, I had a bunch of school books that I felt could do without their pages. Only problem was that security would most likely notice me opening a book cover and making merchandise magically disappear.

I needed to solve this riddle quickly because I was running low on money. I already had my next move in mind that would put me back on top.

A department store at the Chula Vista mall had silver and gold-plated necklaces hanging from a small, squared, rotating display that sat atop a glass jewelry case near the center of the store. That loot was always out of the question because of its wide open location, but I always wanted to get those. They averaged $100 to $200, and I knew I could get $40 to $80 a piece at school.

I ended up cutting the pages out completely from my social studies and physical science books. I then cut pieces of cardboard strips that fit the dimensions of the pages from both books. They were then secured to the inside of the back covers with some rubber cement and left to dry. I glued white strips of paper over the cardboard to give it a more book-like appearance.

Once all that was dry, I cut out large pieces from the back of the social studies book cover and then did the same to the front cover of the physical science book. I sealed the cover of the physical science book closed through its now wide open cover. The social studies book was then placed atop the other and secured with glue. Now I had a convincing looking stack of school books that were completely hollow.

As legit as it looked, this wouldn't help me with the necklaces I wanted. I stared at the cover of my new creation for a bit wondering how I could better it. The social studies book had a small photograph of a hummingbird pictured in flight that was bordered with a thin square. *Then it came to me.*

My dad was a do-it-yourself kind of guy. So we had plenty of tools, hardware, and various materials for quick fixes around the house. I started my search and found all I needed. I'm about to sound like MacGyver right here—or a meth addict. But I gathered a stapler, two medium thickness rubber bands, a cabinet hinge, and a box cutter.

I lightly cut along the square's inner border surrounding the hummingbird with the box cutter, making sure to keep all cuts thin, nice, and straight. Once the hummingbird was removed, about a three-inch square, I opened the cover, lined the piece back up where it would have normally been, and secured the cabinet hinge to connect the small loose piece of cover to its original body with some excess rubber cement, on the inside. I continued by cutting the rubber bands and stapling the two strips from one side of the inner cover to the other.

Now my double hollow school book had a trap door. The rubber bands on the inside would allow the door to be pushed in and then snap back into place, leaving the book cover looking flush outside.

I took my new creation with me to the mall the very next day, and it worked like a charm.

I would position myself in front of the glass jewelry display case and the smaller squared display case that rested atop. Then I would place my hollowed book on its side vertically and keep my right hand gripping the top with the trap door facing the smaller display. I would turn the display slightly so the corner was facing me and adjust the position of my hollowed book to form a V groove with the top of the V facing me. Now I had a small blind spot. All this was done in a slow, steady manner as I pretended to be looking at items in the glass display.

Once I was in position, I would then focus my interest on the necklaces. Removing around ten at a time with one finger, then holding them up to the light for the camera to see that they were in my hand. When my hand came down and back into the blind spot I would quickly tilt my finger down slightly and allow three to four necklaces to fall off before placing the rest back on their display. I remained in my little V groove and would then push my new necklaces through the trap door with my left hand, never coming near the red flag areas.

This book gambit literally never failed me for as long as I used it. Along with a few other small hustles, I was able to keep new stylish clothes on my back, put money in my pocket, and have fun while doing it, until I was about sixteen.

Of course, my mom would notice my new apparel and sometimes ask where I got it. I would usually tell her one of my friends loaned it to me for a while. Having doubts I'm sure, my mother hit me with one of the most gangster sayings I know of: "Don't do the crime, if you can't do the time!" I had heard this many times over the years and knew it was meant as a deterrent for crime.

Only this time I perceived it as a challenge. I knew I could do the time if I was to ever be put in that spot. To me it meant know the risk of what you're doing. Decide if it's worth it, and if you elect to do it and get cracked by the cops, no snitching! I loved that saying.

When Kevin jumped off the gravy train of theft, Olaf, Boomer, Roger, Hunter, and I became closer. All of us were extremely money motivated, with the exception of Hunter. He always seemed to be unwilling to actually participate in our heists. I chalked it up to him having already served two separate stints at a boys' camp by the time he was fourteen.

To be honest, I preferred him not participating with us because he seemed to suck at crime and had proven so twice by being caught. He was, by all accounts, a Dodo bird. He was also the last addition to our tight circle. I had always remained just a little skeptical of him and his loyalty. Not for having been busted twice, but simply because of his personality. He seemed a little sketchy, but there was nothing to prove so at the time. So in the circle he remained.

We perfected our shoplifting pattern. The guy inside the store would wear a walkie-talkie earphone. The watchers would be outside alerting the inside guy if security was waiting outside a door. You see, the inside guy (usually me) never knew who might be waiting on the other side of the door, like our Kmart caper. We'd usually hit Sears because it was on the edge of the mall. Out the door to the parking lot and we'd be on a residential street in the ready car in no time.

If the outside watchers gave the all-clear signal in the earphone, I'd take one last look around and head out to the car with the loot—like colognes and perfumes, watches, shavers, whatever was on our buyers' wish lists. I took some leather jackets for a while until store security started putting those locking cords on them.

One time I snagged a master key to the Guess watch case. We were in a store that was going out of business, and the key was just sitting in the locked case. I tried it on a Guess case at another mall, and sure enough, it worked. We eventually had to drive over fifty miles to Riverside to hit the malls there using our Guess key because of how often we were targeting our own local stores. By the way, a $100 watch would sell for $30.

As we were going on our journeys to the mall or any of our other targeted locations, our paths usually took us through enemy grounds in Chula Vista. Taking the bus wouldn't help avoid many threats simply because the enemies took the bus too.

We'd ride or walk in pairs, usually carrying pocket knives in an attempt to avoid being jumped.

I myself was still not a member of Otay, but it didn't matter. If trouble found one of my friends, it found me, and vice versa.

All five of us would end up attending the same school between 1998 and 2000. The S.A.I.L.S. program—the Sweetwater Academy for Individual Learning Styles. It was a year-round secondary school option for those who appeared unable to keep up with the traditional teaching practices provided by the school district.

I was still roughly six months behind in credits from where I needed to be when I was first enrolled at S.A.I.L.S. But I was caught up in no time. The hours were noon to 6:00 p.m., and the teachers were a big help. Our new school may have looked like a combination of the *Dangerous Minds* and *187* casts, but the program itself was amazing.

There was just one catch. The new program was located on the same property as the Chula Vista Adult School. Our classes were held in trailers at the back of the school campus. That created a small problem since we were now attending school behind enemy lines. So we always stayed on our toes. It was during the year and a half or so I attended this school that I was recruited, or better yet, talked into joining the ranks of a gang.

6
THEIR SHIT IS MY SHIT

EVENTUALLY, POVERTY, DRUGS, dead bodies, and friends encouraged me to join a gang.

Most gang members had very large families whose members were part of a gang. So as a kid, you see everything going on, and even look up to an older brother or cousin. Nine times out of ten, young guys didn't have a dad around because he was in prison. Something was missing in their lives.

When Dad comes out of prison, guys hear the stories either at home or while visiting friends. I had a well-structured, hard-working family, but I was still exposed to the same factors as my friends—in their homes, on the streets, at school, on the bus.

I like to say our neighborhood was a lot like prison, except there were girls. Think about it. By the time I got to prison, I was already fucking used to that life. Dog eat dog.

Inside or out, the gang rules. With their own rules and organization. You know who's in control.

In California, for example, gangs can be motivated to make profound change. Drive-by shootings, for example, were bringing too much attention from the Feds who'd come knocking at the door. But the cops couldn't really do anything until Hispanic gangs came together and made a rule: no drive-by shootings. If you get arrested for one and end up in county or state prison, you will die. By the hand of the gangs inside.

So Hispanic gang members put a stop to the Hispanic drive-bys and policed themselves. They also said no to rapes, child abuse or molestation, no sex crimes of any kind. No bueno. If you did those types of crimes, gangs wouldn't accept you either.

Was I expected to join a gang? No. But it was just clear that those were the ones who seemed to have it the easiest. If you joined, nobody messed with members or their families, and you'd be protected.

One day after school, Hunter and I attended a small house party hosted by an older homie from Otay. Hunter had been a member of the hood for about a year and had known me before joining the gang. I would regularly attend this type of get-together since three of my closest friends were now members and would often invite me along.

The host of the party whom we'll call Art was a very in-shape and all around large motherfucker. He was still on parole after having served a few years in state prison for a shooting. All us kids looked up to him, and most others just fucking feared him.

Hunter and I ended up having a solo conversation with our host at some point. After introductions we heard some of his prison stories. They sounded completely awesome and fucked up to me at the same time.

After the stories Art looked at me and suddenly asked in a very serious manner, "Why aren't you from the hood?" He continued with, "I've seen you around the hood forever and always see you with the homies, so why ain't you from the hood?"

Hunter looked at me with eyes that said, "I'm sorry, you're gonna die." Oh fucking great, I thought. I got the biggest motherfucker in South San Diego asking me why I'm not from his gang and he doesn't look too happy.

I was about 6 foot at that time, but weighed in around a buck fifty-five soaking wet. I remember hoping for no permanent damage and that I didn't stay unconscious for too long if he were to decide to crush me.

I answered with, "I don't know, I'm just not."

Art didn't murder me but asked, "Why not though?"

I didn't have a response. He then asked, "If your homie Hunter here were to get in some shit with the enemies and you were there, would you leave him behind?"

"FUCK NO!" I promptly responded.

"Would you leave Olaf and Boomer behind?"

"FUCK NO!"

Art just looked at me shaking his head in agreement and said, "Then you may as well be from Otay if you're gonna be in the middle of the shit anyway, right?"

He had a point, I remember thinking to myself. He had mad respect in the hood, and I was actually honored that he was the one asking me. I thought to myself for a few seconds, looked at him and said, "You're right."

Art smiled and shook my hand. "That's right, homie! Otay gang!"

Hunter looked pleased at my answer, reached over for a handshake, and said, "Hell yeah, homie, you're from the hood!"

Before this I had never been seriously asked to be from the hood—only the occasional joking question from my friends about when I was going to get it over with and join.

Art was absolutely right, I was always with my friends, and their shit was my shit. I informed Olaf and Boomer later in the evening of the events that had transpired earlier at the party. They were both psyched to hear the news. We celebrated with taking a few spray cans and some liquor out on the town that night, just hoping we ran into enemies.

Even though I was on a probationary period known as "backing up the hood," we left our hood, and our names, in spray-paint anywhere we saw fit. We were close, like brothers. We spent our next few years protecting each other, getting girls, hustling, dodging cops, and smashing any enemies that attempted to mess with us.

By my eighteenth birthday I had only two minor charges and convictions against me: a misdemeanor obstruction of justice at fifteen, and a vandalism charge at seventeen. My obstruction of justice charge was from a couple of officers that attempted to detain me in front of my residence for suspicion of possessing a firearm, they later claimed. I didn't stick around long enough for them to finish their commands upon their approach and proceeded to hall ass out of there.

Around four blocks, three fences, and a shocked Mom later, they caught up to me on Melrose and Main near the river bottom. As I long suspected, they weren't too thrilled about running, so I caught an unnecessary takedown with the side of my face impacting the concrete followed by a knee to the back and the bottom of a shiny black shoe firmly pinning my head. Cuffs were put on, I was informed of how stupid I was, and I was off to kid jail to be stripped down naked for a grown ass man during the intake process.

Turned out I was right all along, and getting arrested was no bueno. They found no firearm, which I actually never even had, and let me go the following night with the misdemeanor charge of obstruction.

The vandalism I may have had coming. A friend and I were walking down Orange Avenue coming from the direction of Castle Park High and heading to another friend's house off of Anita Street around two or three in the morning. My friend was leaving his mark about anywhere he could with black spray-paint. It was the same thing every time: Otay RBLs, followed by his moniker.

We reached our destination, did whatever it was that needed doing, and headed back to our starting point. Upon our walk back along Orange Avenue, we noticed two patrol cars racing toward us with their headlights off. At this point my friend may or may not have had a gun in his waistband, I can't recall. The cops had the jump on us, and we knew what we had to do. Only this time I realized I couldn't focus on number one. If my friend got caught with the theoretical firearm, with him being eighteen, he's getting broke off at least a few years.

We were both headed to the same fence at the same time when the patrol cars pulled up slamming on their brakes. A police officer hopped out from each car drawing and then aiming their firearms and shouting, "STOP, POLICE! GET DOWN ON THE GROUND!"

I had to make a decision. Keep going and hope they don't catch us in the search of the surrounding area, or let my friend get away clean while I hold the police back. I probably wouldn't even catch a charge, I remember thinking to myself.

My friend disappeared over the fences, and I stopped at the fence line. I had a plan. I elected to antagonize and confuse the officers a little. I stopped in my tracks a few feet away from the fence, turned to face the officers, who were still shielded behind their patrol car doors with guns drawn, and I began to run around in a roughly ten-foot-diameter circle while making noises that sounded something like, "HOOH-HAH-HEH," stopping once to act as though I was going to make a break for it, then continuing two more laps before finally stopping, throwing my hands up in the air, and blankly staring at the officers.

They shifted their aim from me, to the fence line my friend had disappeared over, and back again, in a rapid, confused manner. Then finally guns settled on me. I don't know why I acted like an escaped mental patient, but it happened, and it was effective.

Turns out they were on Orange with their headlights off because they had noticed my friend's calling card written in paint along their travels. When he hit the fence, the spray can was left behind, and I was subsequently charged and convicted for vandalism. I took the insignificant rap, no problem.

My parents moved to a home in Los Angeles County just before my eighteenth birthday. They were getting a bigger house in a better area along with a raise for transferring their jobs. Their dreams were coming true.

But there was nothing for me in Los Angeles I figured. No friends, no girls, no connections, no crime partners, no money. I would have a place to stay and be with family, but that would be it. I knew my hustle options would be limited, so I elected to remain in San Diego living with my close friend Boomer. A dumb teenage move, I know.

By this time we were getting by primarily on petty thefts, car burglaries, and grand theft autos. It wasn't always cutting it though. We stayed in a back house on property owned by Boomer's grandparents in a rural area of Bonita.

Bonita is a beautiful place, but this back house sure as hell wasn't, as much as I appreciated the opportunity to live there and all. It was uninhabited for many years prior to us moving in. No big deal about the peeling paint and run-down features, but I was more concerned about what kind of creatures were living there with us.

We equipped a 250-square-foot living area with bunk beds, one recliner, and a mini fridge. A working bathroom had random rattlesnakes to go with. The small, attached garage was filled from top to bottom with contents the grandparents had acquired over several decades during their still thriving marriage. It wasn't much, but we called it our command post.

Neither of us had a car, and we now lived in the middle of nowhere, by our own standards anyway. Since parking a stolen car in Boomer's grandparents' driveway wasn't an option, we'd have to hoof it most places.

My mom agreed to help me get a car if I landed a job. So I applied to a local UPS and got a spot loading and unloading. I had to work for a few months to save enough for the down payment, but in no time I was cruising around in an awesome 1999 Buick Regal. It was a newer model car so pulling girls was not a problem. We would hit Highland Avenue in National City frequently.

On weekends at around 8:00 p.m. Highland would be bumper to bumper with sick, pimped-out low riders equipped with flashy rims, decorative color lights emanating from beneath some vehicles, and loud sound systems, cruising in both directions.

Other vehicles would also be in attendance, but the cars with the best rims, paint jobs, and sound systems stole the show—and the girls usually. Masses of people lined the street on both sides of Highland for just over a mile-long stretch. We would only put gangster shit in the CD player during our cruising sessions and let our presence be known at a high volume. 2Pac's "Lil' Homies" was always a favorite. My CD collection was a thing of beauty, with most disks consisting of all the best West Coast rappers at the time.

Looking out the car window and into the glare of the streetlights, I would see girls looking fine as fuck in next to nothing, people waving the Mexican flag, with others just socializing and having fun and enjoying each other's company in front of the scattered storefronts. It was a weekly parade for people from all neighborhoods to enjoy—my favorite time of the week. I loved cruising!

Yet the one pastime I loved even more than cruising was stealing. I had improved my skills over the years and came to enjoy the act very much. Car thefts were simple. I had invested in a dent puller, spring-activated center punch, and a hacksaw. Any car that had one of those red clubs that locked on the steering wheel was first on the list. We knew they more than likely had no alarm system in place, and the steering wheel was easy to cut through. We would be in someone's car and gone with it in under two minutes. It was fun, challenging, and a rush.

If we weren't stealing someone's car, we were stealing someone's van or motorcycle. The van would actually be stolen in order to get the motorcycle later. It was only a dead-of-night type of activity though. We would obtain work vans that had no rear seating and then cruise around looking for a new bike to snatch up. Once we found one, we'd quickly pull alongside it, exit the vehicle, and promptly lift the motorcycle up and into the van.

Then it was straight back to the homie's house with our new bike. We would repaint the motorcycle and try to sell it later. We almost never stole cars from our own hood. I only recall it happening once, and out of pure laziness.

During one of these paint jobs, we were interrupted by the homie's mom. She had arrived home from a late night out and realized exactly what we were doing. She knew what was up but decided to lay some game on us. She immediately began to inform the four of us (bouncing between both English and Spanish) of exactly how stupid she believed we were.

Once the insults subsided, she then asked, "Will this even pay for the bail if you get caught? How 'bout the attorney?"

Holy fucking shit, she was right, I thought to myself. We were having fun, but the risk far outweighed the reward. We needed to think of a bigger, better plan and leave that petty shit alone and behind us. We continued with our petty thefts, but all the while plotted what our big move should be.

And that turned into bank robbery.

7
SEASON OF SUCCESS

ALL FOR A Taco Bell grande meal, I had proposed we hit a bank. And we did.

My "SMILE" note went over well. I had stuffed stacks of bills into a Carl's Junior bag with some stray, dried-out fries, quickly if not confidently raced out of the bank branch and into the waiting, stolen getaway car, safely switched to our legit car in the neighborhood, dodged any cops, and hit it back to my homie's house.

We peeked out the closed blinds for peace of mind before dumping the money out of the crumpled paper bag onto the living room floor and counting the bounty.

We had almost $8,000 by the time we were done. Fuck working! That was the kind of paycheck I wanted every week! We divided the cash equally three ways. All of us would catch the same charges if we were to be caught, we figured. So equal risks deserved equal rewards.

While the money still sat in three separate piles on the living room floor, we heard a knock on the door. Holy shit! Who the fuck could that be, the fucking cops? Our host approached the door cautiously, slowly looking out the peephole. It was just one of our other close friends who hadn't been made aware of our last-minute scheme, arriving to see what we were up to.

He was pulled in with our host closing the door quickly behind him. He looked down to the floor and directly at the three piles of cash. "What the fuck? What did you guys do?" He wasn't concerned that we had obviously committed some sort of crime. He was just simply curious as to how this cash came to be here and was immediately demanding an explanation as to why he wasn't invited along for the ride.

"It was a two-door G-ride," I explained. "You wouldn't fit." A G-ride is a stolen car, a gangster ride.

This was true but also a lie. The getaway car was in fact a two-door, but we didn't have any other available positions. Three was all that was needed. One to go in, one to drive and keep lookout, and finally one for the legit ride. He didn't like my explanation and dismissed it as bullshit. I told him we could rotate for all I cared. I only wanted to get paid, and I had found a way to do just that. We told our depressed friend that he would be more than welcome to participate in our next heist if he was still interested when that time came. He agreed, but still didn't seem too happy.

Well fuck him. I was happy as shit. I had "made" almost three grand in a single day, and I was ecstatic. I hit the Plaza Bonita Mall that night and loaded up on some new clothes, shoes, cologne, a watch, and a couple yellow-gold rings to add some class to my new outfits. The next day I was itching to cruise around the hood with the homies in order to floss on, then effectively pick up some girls.

I knew myself and my two bank-robbery friends wouldn't have any problems doing so, but our still depressed and very indigent homie might have some trouble. I creased up a light brown short-sleeved button-up shirt (only on the sleeves). Then worked on a pair of new black Tommy Hilfiger jeans, which were purchased ten sizes larger than I actually needed in order to achieve two folds at the front as though they were pleated. Next I unboxed some new tan Lugz, slid those motherfuckers on, and then capped it off with my two gold rings and a black lambskin leather jacket from Wilsons.

Looking like a Miami-based drug dealer, I was ready to hit the hood. I still had about half of my earnings left after my shopping trip, so flossing on some *hynas* (Hispanic girls) was definitely on the table. I called up one of my accomplices and asked if he knew of any parties or kickbacks taking place with a proper balance of titties available. He didn't know of any, so we ultimately decided to throw our own at the Red Lion Inn and Suites in National City. We hit up some girls and told them to roll through if they wanted to chill.

A couple hours after getting the room, we had it filled to capacity with some fine-ass chicks and a few of our trusted friends. Word was starting to spread in our social circle that we had obviously done something big, but no one knew what.

Girls at the hotel party were especially curious as to how I came into my new wealth and would frequently ask questions. I hadn't thought of a cover story to justify my new earnings, so I just told them the most vague and admittedly dumb answer I could have possibly came up with at the time: "I own an internet company," I dimwittedly stated to all who asked. Yet no one really questioned it too much further, and I'm very glad they didn't.

For the next two days there was a rumor going around that I was suddenly a dot.com millionaire. I had girls I didn't even know blowing me up asking if my friends and I wanted to come chill. Within a couple days the rumor was dismissed as bullshit, and everyone just assumed we were pushing large amounts of drugs. Now that I think about it, I actually received more phone calls from girls after the drug rumor began. It was great. Having money and being a fake drug dealer was working out for me just fucking fine.

It was only a couple weeks before we all ran out of our newly acquired proceeds. All of us knew we needed to hit another bank. We decided to carry out our new heist in a different area with the hopes of throwing off the cops.

We settled on a bank in Mission Valley, which lies about seventeen miles north of Otay. The decision was made to steal the next getaway car from a different city than where the bank was located. This would ensure that our G-ride would not be on the hot list of the local PD in the area of our planned caper.

We went out that night and snatched up an inconspicuous ride and parked it where we would be switching out cars after the robbery the following day. The switch-off location was only blocks from the bank, and parking it there would help us avoid any unnecessary driving of the stolen ride the next day.

I have to admit, I was still a little nervous. We knew our plan was pretty solid, but also knew that cops get lucky sometimes. No sense in second guessing it, the next morning it was on. It was time to get paid again.

I carried out my hat and glasses bundled up in a hooded sweat shirt to the getaway car to avoid neighbors possibly seeing my apparel on the news later. I threw Mack 10's "Bang or Ball" in the CD player, put it on "Hate in Yo Eyes," and we all headed toward the bank.

No note this time. I had decided to recite my lines to the teller in hopes of it speeding up the process. We arrived at the switch-off location where our G-ride was still parked, and I hopped in the ride with Ned. Bob again stayed behind in the legit ride, and we were off to handle business.

We pulled into the parking lot of the bank with Brotha Lynch's "Season of Da Siccness" playing at a mild volume. Brotha Lynch was always a preferred choice when we needed to pump ourselves up with some good beats and sick-ass lyrics.

I instructed the homie to park as close to the door as possible since I was planning on being quick. We reversed into the spot and parked, and I was out of the car and into the bank with the quickness.

This time I skipped waiting in line and went straight up to the teller, excusing myself to the patrons who had been waiting patiently for their turn. I stood face-to-face with the teller and began to say my lines at a somewhat rapid pace: "Put the money on the counter. No ink packs, alarms, or tracing devices. There's two more guys outside with guns. Hurry up, this ain't no joke."

She complied immediately and began placing the money on the counter. As she was stacking the green goodness on the counter, I scanned the interior area for any heroes while my driver watched the outside of the premises with his cell phone in hand to alert me of any emergencies. I got a little cocky and demanded that the teller give me the rest of the drawers. She stated that she couldn't, as she didn't have the necessary keys to unlock another employee's drawer.

I paused for a few seconds wondering if she was trying to play me. I realized it didn't matter as I literally planned on doing nothing but leaving if I were to ever hit any resistance from a teller. So I grabbed the money, bent all stacks to feel for the ink packs, and placed them in my bag. Once the money was all collected, I exited the bank, hopped in the car, and drove back to the switch-off location.

We pulled up at a steady pace and parked in front of a house around the corner from the legit ride. As we were walking to the second car, an SUV pulled up with two larger white guys inside. They immediately began cursing at both of us, and the passenger demanded that we get the car we had just parked away from his mom's house. He seemed to understand that something wasn't right with the situation.

We continued to walk as though we didn't know what the fuck they were talking about. Which only irritated them more. Turns out they were skinheads and identified themselves as such.

We didn't really have to wait for them to identify themselves through all the racially motivated obscenities like "beaners" and "spics" they were hurling our way. Dealing with the Alt Right was not factored into the plan at all, and we were confused on how to proceed.

We paused for a sec making eye contact with Bob, whom we now had a clear sight of. He realized what was happening and shouted for us to hurry the fuck up. There was no option of a gang fight at that moment, too much on the line, so we just ran to the legit car and dipped out (left quickly).

The skinheads stayed in pursuit until we lost them on the freeway, but turned out they never gave any critical info to the cops.

We cruised back to the hood and got to counting. I don't remember how much we scored that time, somewhere around $5,000, I believe. What I did notice is that it was much easier and faster to just verbally demand the money. Doing it that way had me in and out in under two minutes. I practiced my lines often, whenever I had moments of time to myself.

I had decided one teller wasn't worth the risk, I wanted them all. My goal was to be able to say my lines up to five times faster with no hiccups. Turned out three times was the magic number. I could say, "Put the money on the counter. No ink packs, alarms, or tracing devices. There's two more guys outside with guns. Hurry up, this ain't no joke!" three times, clearly, with pauses between tellers included in the timing, in about fifteen seconds.

Which meant if the tellers complied with my demands quickly, I could be in and out in under a minute, three times as rich, and the tellers would have an interesting story to tell their families and friends for some time to come. A win, win.

8
IT'S GOING DOWN

A WEEK AFTER our last hit I was ready to put my timed talk theory to the test, and I had the perfect bank in mind. I had basically been scoping that spot out for years. For some completely fucktarded reason, my teenage mind had settled on robbing my mom's credit union. To play it safe, I would wear an oversized hooded sweat shirt with my hat and glasses to better mask my identity. I had visited that bank for years as a child and teenager with my mom.

I knew their drawers were stacked, and getting away wouldn't be a problem. All three of us were familiar with the area. The bank was located on Palm Avenue just one freeway exit or a riverbed away from my neighborhood. Police at the time would not follow anyone into the riverbed due to the possibility of being ambushed there by suspects. The river weeds would grow thick, over six feet tall, and the water and mud would act as a cloak to avoid chopper detection too. It was the perfect hiding area if things were to go south during the hit. I ran my co-conspirators down on my selection, and we all agreed it would be next on the list.

We went through our normal procedure of acquiring a car the night before in a different jurisdiction and went to sleep a little early so we could be at the bank first thing, bright-eyed and bushy-tailed.

The next morning it was time to rock and roll. We went over our foot pursuit escape plan and noted where the pick-up location would be for that scenario. We also explored some alternate car chase routes, just to be on the safe side, you know?

Once all precautionary measures were covered, we took a short cruise over to the bank. The legit ride would stay parked off the main street exit near the Boys and Girls Club this time. The freeway wasn't a concern in this case since police response time sucked balls back then. We knew we could hit the bank, clear the area, and be counting the money back at home in about ten minutes from start to finish.

We pulled up to the credit union and parked in a space near the front entrance. I hopped out and casually walked inside, trying my best to not look like a straight up burn. I approached the teller with a smile on my face, said, "Excuse me," and proceeded to say my lines.

Everything went perfect, including a smooth getaway. I was wrong on my timing though. We were counting our money at the pad only seven minutes after I first entered the bank. I believe we ended up with something to the tune of $8,000. Upon that realization, I had made up my mind: I would rob banks forever, fuck work.

To celebrate my latest victory, I had decided to buy myself a TV for the ride. I cruised over to Good Guys to browse around and found a nice seven-inch for the dash and a sound system to go with. I paid cash money, and not too much later, I was riding around watching movies on the go, bumping (playing music with bass). Rims soon followed. I topped it off with some interior neon lighting and a PlayStation 2. Oh yeah, my shit was sick.

I was being somewhat loose with my cash and needed to check how I was doing on funds. I got home and opened up the safe. Jesus Christ, I was running low. Too fucking low. I checked my pockets for any loose hundreds and fifties but only found my damn rim receipt. I was down to around $800. I threw the receipt in the safe, took my last $800 out, and went cruising, angrily. I can't keep being this careless with my money, I remember thinking.

By this time I'd been out of school for a few years. I'd gotten my GED after leaving the alternative school just before graduation. I'd been working at UPS and then as a security guard for Pinkerton. It was a temp job, night gigs. I never carried a gun, just a clipboard. When they asked me to sit in front of an elevator and watch for some bad dude (here's his picture on the clipboard), I realized this wasn't a job for me. A clipboard wasn't enough protection against potentially armed bad guys.

I had to get a plan together that I could invest in, for my own future. But before I could do that, I needed to find a bank I could rob. I needed money for whatever this future investment of mine was going to be. So I started the search for our next target by cruising around.

Shortly into my drive, I received a call from a couple homies we'll call Charlie B and Clayface. They asked me if I wanted to go hitting up with them in the enemy's neighborhood (tagging). I told them I was down and asked where they were. They shot me their location, and I headed that way. I scooped them up and began our drive toward Woodlawn, bumping Brotha Lynch.

A couple hours and several spray-painted walls later, Charlie B says he needs to take a shit, and badly at that!

"There's nothing open," I told him. It was three in the morning. "You gotta wait till we get back to the hood and I'll drop you off."

He said he couldn't wait and frantically demanded for me to, "PULL OVER, NOW, FUCKER."

I pulled over then and there. We were on a residential street and naturally landed next to a small house. There was a car in the driveway and no lights on.

Charlie B ran his ass in great haste to the backside of the car (facing us and away from the house), dropped his wind breakers, and shit on this poor motherfucker's driveway. Clayface and I were busting up at Charlie B. He had no shame.

Then, out of nowhere, the porch light comes on and some pudgy middle-aged Hispanic guy starts heading out in a hurry. Charlie B had pinched off maybe half a loaf and began heading back almost immediately when the lights popped on, pulling his wind breakers up as he fumbled his way back to the car. He slid in the backseat through the door he had left open, and we made our escape, laughing at Charlie B's expense our whole way back to the hood.

Planning my next hit could wait for the following day.

The next afternoon I pitched the idea of another hit to my squad over the phone, and, as usual, they were down. We decided on a day that was soon approaching so we could all be available and included in the heist. I took on the task of finding our new location and headed straight to the car after our conversation. It was hot as fuck that day. I remember thinking to myself that my leather seats were going to be scorching.

I unlocked the ride, which was parked in the sun, hopped inside, and immediately rolled down all the windows to let the heat out. Of course, the seats were hot as shit. But something smelled horrible, I mean, death horrible. I started looking for any old food that may have baked in the sun but couldn't spot anything out of the norm, until I looked at my backseat.

Charlie B had put a nice brown streak of shit across my whole backseat when he slid in and just got dropped off saying nothing about it. Sick fucker. So off to get my car detailed I went and, along the way, found my next bank.

What I spotted was a bank in a perfect spot (for getaway purposes), somewhat close to the hood (but not so close as to draw attention), with an average of three tellers working a day, and stacked drawers. This was a damn good bank, but it was literally my bank. I handled my car loan directly through that place at the time. So when I was there making my payments, I saw the drawers filled with bills and watched where the teller put my money as well.

I quickly concluded that my hat and glasses with a baggy hoodie should do just fine for concealing my true identity—one of their own customers. I even brought my own bag, a clear grocery bag, so people could see the money I was walking away with. A wanted poster shows the robber with a disguise and carrying a clear plastic bag with $22,000 in it.

I'm not sure that's me on the wanted poster.

I pitched this bank to the homies. They asked if I was sure, and I remained confident in my decision. It was two days until go time. I was pumped up.

The next morning, with one day to go, we found out a member of our squad had won an all-expenses paid vacation extravaganza package from the state and would be unable to join us on our future missions. This was bad news to hear. Not only was he from the hood, he was a member of our squad.

The other homie's girlfriend took this as a sign of bad luck and forbid him from taking part in the following day's hit. He fucking listened to her superstitious self. I was left on my own like a fart in the wind. So I reached out to another long-term friend (whom we'll call Crash), a somewhat high-strung homie, but he was like my brother, and one of the most solid people I've ever met. So I asked him to help me out.

Once I ran him down on the hustle and my next target location, he paused briefly and said, "I fucking knew you guys were up to something like this. Why didn't you tell me sooner?"

I explained that he was a cripple and would be unable to run on foot if shit went south. So the other guys, not me, voted against him. He swore to secrecy and we went on our own. We parked my ride in the switch-off location and headed over to our next stop in a 1980-something Honda Civic with no driver waiting in the legit ride watching the main streets.

Crash was driving erratically from time to time due to his handicap, a thought also considered in our voting system, but nevertheless we arrived on location. I was a little rattled from the ride over, but safe, and still dedicated.

I went in with high hopes and hungry pockets, but got one fucking teller on duty and an uptight looking one at that. Fuck, I hope she's packing a fat drawer, I remember thinking. I said my lines, looking behind me frequently at a few customers who were patiently waiting their turn as I myself waited for her to finish putting the money on the counter.

She announced, "That's it."

I looked and saw a pretty tall pile of twenties on the counter and proceeded to put them in my bag while again checking my surroundings and then made a quick exit. We sped off in reckless haste with Crash asking me, "How much do you think we got?"

I told him it was maybe $6,000 and for the love of God to please slow the fuck down. We eventually arrived back to the spot where my car was parked.

He took over that driving gig as well. We hit side streets back to the hood and made it home in no time. Once we got inside, he asked to see the money. I handed him the bag and excused myself to the restroom to take an overdue piss. Exiting the restroom and back to the living room I see Crash looking at our loot.

"This fucking bank carries a lot of fives and tens," he stated as I walked back in the living room.

"What do you mean?" I asked. I walked over to the pile of cash that was now scattered across the coffee table and realized that the damn uptight fucking teller played me. She must have given me the petty cash drawer and sprinkled twenties atop a bunch of smaller bills while I was checking my surroundings. I'd been swindled. What the fuck is up with people?

We had about $1,300 total. This was all bad. I couldn't rob banks for six hundred and fifty fucking dollars a pop. I explained to Crash that this typically doesn't happen and that she just simply got over on us. He reluctantly accepted it and took his half of the money, shoving it in his pocket and proceeded to watch the news for any signs of our caper.

I couldn't build my future around hundreds of dollars. While lying back in the sofa and staring at my large pile of small bills, I asked Crash, "Wanna hit another bank this week?"

Without even looking away from the television, he said, "Well yeah. I'm down. Fuck it."

By this time, the Feds knew there was a spree robber on the loose. Actually, there were two of us. The Pale-Faced Bandit was doing some of his own with similar techniques to mine. But he fucked up and got caught trying to launder, literally, his ink-stained bills at a casino. He didn't know how to check for ink packs inside the stacks.

He was tracked on casino security cameras loading the stained bills into the slot machines and then cashing out with freshly laundered casino money. I too used casinos to cash out, literally, because I worried that they would be tracking serial numbers.

Three days later I was running back up in my mom's bank for a second time.

I continued hitting banks that were randomly picked during cruising sessions over the next several months, getting more cocky and faster on my in-and-out times as we progressed. I'd approach three tellers, one by one, give my spiel down the line, and head back to teller number one and start loading up the money in my clear bag. Media began writing articles and airing reports on my adventures over the news frequently.

A newspaper article headlined, "Not a Thin Dime for the Skinny Bandit," but that wasn't me that time.

I got so big headed, or stupid, that I actually hit a bank, rolled up the sleeves on my long-sleeved shirt, took off my hat and glasses, and went down to the courthouse (where damn near every local news station was present for a highly publicized murder trial), walked past everyone, and proceeded to pay a court fine with the money I had recently acquired.

Now that's another story: that fine was for misdemeanor trespassing. I had missed my court date. Now how could that happen when the sheriff had three full days to take me from jail to the courthouse right across the street? It happened because the sheriff put me on an elevator to the underground walkway, and with forty people onboard, the damn thing got stuck. We were packed in there, nuts to butts in the first place, so shorter people started passing out. The walls were dripping with sweat and condensation from our breathing or inability to.

We prisoners aboard used our county jail sandals to try to pry the doors open and hold them there, just to get air. About six hours later, the fire department arrived. Took their fucking time. In this case, it caused me to miss my court date (not my fault, but the sheriff's), and the judge could only give me a fine, which I happily paid with my recent earnings.

The Skinny Bandit is what they dubbed me. Fucking assholes. Don't they know it's wrong to shame a teenager about their weight? Yet, with all the dumb-ass teenage decisions I had made along the way, no one ever recognized me. Not at my mom's bank (either time), not at my bank, not from the news. That is, until I got lazy.

9
FOR THE LOVE OF MONEY

I BEGAN ROBBING banks even when I didn't need to. I was becoming addicted to not only the money, but the planning and the thrill. We had a system down that no law enforcement agency seemed to be able to keep up with. I knew I was being full of myself, but I felt I'd earned that through all my efforts. One day I was asked if I'd plan out and take part in a bank hit to help someone out who needed funds desperately and was down to put in work for it.

I agreed and told the homie in need to go out with me that night to look for a G-ride and we'd hit the bank the next day. He seemed a little unnerved by how soon it went from him asking for a favor to it's now happening in a matter of hours, but he was still down. He suggested we steal a car from the hood (his comfort zone), and I lazily agreed. I knew it was against our protocol, but simply didn't feel like searching for a new car lot.

We parked my ride on Second Avenue and went walking down the long street that was lined with cars under dim streetlights on both sides. I favored Mustangs, Hondas, and Acuras. I could get a Mustang in under thirty seconds with a center punch and dent puller. A master key I had for Acuras and Hondas made those thefts even quicker.

We eventually came across a Honda. I put my master key in the door's keyhole and began to work my magic. A few flicks of the locks later and we were in. We shuffled through things real quick, just to check for valuables, and possibly a spare key. A real key always beat a master key because there's no jiggling and sawing motions needed.

I flipped down the passenger side visor and didn't find anything there except for a small sticker with a photo on it of two girls cheek to cheek. They were around my age, it seemed. I looked for a brief moment and told the homie, "One of these chicks looks familiar." He looked, I looked again, and we eventually just flipped up the visor and shrugged it off. I chalked it up to the fact that she just had one of those faces. I put the master key in the ignition, did my thing, and we were off.

We hit the bank the following day without a hiccup. Proper procedures were followed, and we were a little richer than we had originally been the day before.

I moved on with my week like it had just been another day at the office. It was during this week I believe that I received a knock on the door—a homie from the hood, and he had news, good news according to him.

"Congratulations, doggy. They caught the Skinny Bandit!" he announced.

I told him he should quit using drugs ASAP unless he's been undercover since infancy and was there to arrest me himself.

He said, "Dog, they got him. That's it, you're retired!" and looked at me as though he didn't understand why the information was so hard for me to wrap my head around. He went on to explain that some guy, my age and apparently my doppelganger, had been arrested at the Palomar trolley station.

Another person also at the trolley stop had been a victim, or witness, to a robbery allegedly committed by the Skinny Bandit. She "recognized" him as being the Skinny Bandit and called the cops from a pay phone. She told them she was sure it was him. He was even wearing clothing similar to what I had been known to wear in my robberies.

I heard this kid got swooped on in the realest way by two or three law enforcement agencies right there at Palomar trolley station and thrown in jail. He denied everything. They interrogated him for hours on end and actually got him to admit he was present at one of the robberies. Why the fuck would he do that, you ask?

Well once they got him and realized our striking similarities, they threw him in every photo lineup possible and presented it to all the tellers that had been hit over the now nine or ten banks in the spree. Most of the tellers identified him as "possibly being the robber."

So the interrogators presented him with this bit of information. One teller in particular was very adamant that he was the guy! The cops asked him something like, "Why would she be so certain it was you?" and he, completely innocent and under hours of interrogation, said, "Maybe I was there around that time and that's why she thinks she recognizes me?" So he now placed himself at the scene of the crime.

Also against him was the fact that he had previously bragged to a girl about how he had just stole a Honda (one of my favorite getaway cars). He had even missed three or so court-ordered appointments that fell on days I hit banks. (LMAO, this guy was fucked.)

Meanwhile, back in Otay, I sipped on a cold bottle of Coke and wondered what I should do with my new clean slate. I could buy and sell drugs! That's always a thriving enterprise, but it is full of drama. I continued to think for a while about different scams I could get into.

A few days later I decided that anything else was far too much stress for me. Robbing banks was where it was at, a winning system, and that's where I wanted to be. I also felt a little bad for the Skinny Bandit's stunt double.

I hit two or three more banks before they finally let that poor bastard go. The prosecutors in the city of San Diego were praised on their conviction rate. Never really known to just let a ghetto kid go and admit fault for a false arrest. Kind of like now I guess. In the process of their royal fuck up and borderline illegal interrogation techniques, they helped me out in a real way.

I would later come to find out that none of those first eight or nine bank witnesses were credible on the stand. They all proved themselves to be uncertain by first identifying the wrong person.

I'd like to take a moment to thank that officer or agent for their mistake there. If you hadn't tried so hard to send the wrong person away, I may have gotten more prison time. Don't go taking all the credit though. I'm sure it was a collaborative effort. So I may as well just say thank you to all agents or officers involved on my case. You may have violated your duties to uphold the law, and completely disregarded due process, *and* may have tried to send an innocent neighborhood teen away, but you got me less time. Much appreciated.

10
WORK HARD, PLAY HARD

I RENTED A motel suite at a La Quinta Inn and Suites in the city of Bonita to throw a little kickback one night. I had Crash and a few girls over for beers. Crash and I were celebrating another successful hit from just one day prior. We were all just chilling (hanging out) watching the news before heading over to Denny's, when a full screen image of *me*, standing in line at my first bank hit, looking straight at the camera, enveloped the entire television screen.

One of the girls did a double take. Looked back at me and said, "That's you!"

I believe the screen read, "Responsible for 13 local bank robberies, FBI seeks public's help." A little off on the numbers, too low, I thought, but I'll take it.

I calmly said to her, "Do you really think I'd be sitting here if I had robbed thirteen banks?" I continued, "I'd be a fucking millionaire."

After a few more Coronas, she let it go. At the end of the night everyone took off home, with the exception of one girl who had elected to stay the night. At around three in the morning I got a call from a friend of the girl lying next to me. Her name was Vicky, and she was a tweaker. Three a.m. calls weren't all that uncommon for her, but if I had paid better attention at the time, I would have realized that the call itself was very unusual.

Vicky asked where her friend was. I said next to me sleeping. She asked who else was there with us. I said no one. She asked where I was, and then asked what room we were in. I answered each question without even thinking anything was up. I figured maybe she and her friend just wanted to take turns sucking my dick—I had hoped anyway. Not the case apparently.

After her rapid-fire questioning she just said, "Okay, bye!" and hung up. Another tweaker moment of hers I thought to myself, and went back to sleep.

That morning, September 22, 2002, I awoke to the sound of loud banging on my motel room door followed by about five voices screaming, "FBI, FBI, OPEN UP!"

I jolted up in bed, with the deepest dread and oh-shit feeling one could possibly have. I paused, looked at the girl next to me, realized her friend had set me up, got up, and just walked to the door. It was all over.

I made the long eight-foot journey from the bed to the door with "FBI, OPEN UP. NOW!" they shouted as I approached the door.

"Hold on, let me get this latch off," I shouted back. I unlocked the door, looked outside and down the barrels of about six handguns, stepped back, and was placed in cuffs.

I asked why they were there. The agent in charge told me it was to serve a search warrant. She was a small, thin lady maybe in her late forties to midfifties with short hair. Looked more like a teacher than a Fed. She, along with a Chula Vista police detective, transported me down to the FBI headquarters in San Diego and began questioning me about the string of robberies.

They wanted me to roll on my associates. That wasn't going to happen. There was no one to roll on, in my opinion. I stated that if I hadn't done anything, then how could anyone else have helped me do the thing for which I had no knowledge, eh? If you can't do the time, don't do the crime. I live by that shit.

Once I realized this was more than just a search warrant issue, I requested to be taken to jail, and they were happy to oblige. They transported me to the Chula Vista police station. From there I was handcuffed to two other individuals, crammed in the back of a patrol car, and taken to San Diego County jail.

While in the back of the car, one of my cuffed-up friends asked what I was arrested for. I told him of the *alleged* charges, and he began to praise me immediately. He was in his midtwenties, had short black hair, no tattoos, and had been occasionally glancing in my direction before initiating his conversation with me.

He frequently commented on how cool my crimes were. He continued by saying he had also been arrested for bank robbery in the past and that he got off easy because he'd confessed from the beginning. I had my suspicions before, with how loud he was talking so close in proximity to a cop while we were standing in line, but now I knew. This dude was an undercover.

I broke all communication with this guy, but he still tried to pry. We arrived at the county jail and were put in the first tank or holding cell of the intake process, but first gave up all our personal items at the reception window. In the tank there was a blue phone attached to a white concrete wall near the end of a metal bench. I jumped on the phone to inform a few people of what had happened.

Soon into my first call, the undercover dip fuck made it a point to sit oddly close to me and my phone call. After the call he tried to strike up conversation again by asking if I had in fact done what they allege, and I again said no. He pressed a few more times, and I stopped answering him entirely. He got the message.

He walked up to the holding tank's metal door and pounded on it. A guard walked up, looked through the door's window, and put his ear to the crack of the door. Undercover fucktard said a few words in a whisper through the crack. The guard unlocked the door and pulled him out. I took that to be confirmation of my suspicions and knew I needed to stay on my toes in there. I decided trusting no one was probably best.

I was optimistic for the most part. I only had twenty dollars on me at the time of my arrest, and they seemed desperate to get me to tell on myself. It seemed as though they didn't have much, so how the fuck did they even get me?

Once I met with my attorney, I realized what led them to me. That fucken Honda from Second Avenue. Turned out I went to school with that girl in the picture on the visor. She knew who I was, and it was her car.

When the cops told her that her car had been used in a bank robbery, she asked if they had a picture of the suspect. They did indeed—in the form of a wanted poster. Upon showing her this wanted poster, she said she thought I looked familiar and proceeded to retrieve her high school yearbook from inside her home. She took the yearbook back outside to the waiting officers and pointed me out. The cops began their investigation on me that day. See what laziness gets you?

Just before my first court appointment, I saw two of my homies being placed in a cell next door to the one I was in. I yelled out the side of the door and asked why they were there. They told me it was for the same charges I myself had.

Turns out the girl I was with at the time of my arrest gave the cops their names as close associates of mine. They allegedly found them both with marked bills from a recent bank robbery I was suspected of carrying out, but neither talked to the cops. Once all charges had been levied against us, I had about twenty counts of bank robbery, two conspiracies, and a car burglary charge (I didn't actually do the car burglary). My associates had the same number of charges, but they were listed as "conspiracy to commit robbery."

One of my associates was found in possession of a safe that contained $17,000, a small amount of drugs, a couple master keys (allegedly for car theft), and a receipt for one set of rims equipped with a signature, my fucking signature. Started not looking too good for ol' Rich at that point.

Until I found out all the details on the arrest that preceded mine. Their fuck up in arresting the lookalike dude took me from looking at damn near life in prison to a deal for six, seven, or eight years (the choice was up to the judge). When I was presented with this deal, I was told all robbery charges would be dropped against my friends and one would be given sixteen months with half, and the other would get two years with half, but I would need to sign then and there.

My mom had already suggested by that point for me to sign for anything under ten years, so I took it. So many young people are put in that same situation but are presented with a get-out-of-jail-free card, but they first have to sign a deal. An example of a deal could be probation with a strike, for possibly a fight. You see if you get arrested for residential burglary, it's considered a violent crime in California.

So a two-year strikeable offense is now doubled up to four if the person has a previous strike, and it is to be served at 85 percent. Then afterward *any* new crime that followed was life in prison if you already had two existing strikes. Even a misdemeanor could be turned into a felony charge if you had two strikes. That's why kids and adults alike sell their souls for their immediate release from custody. Then the system gets them forever. It's designed for people who can't afford bail or a paid attorney.

At sentencing I received the max allowed under the deal: eight years, with two strikes, and no less than 85 percent of my sentence to be served before my release. I was nineteen years old and tried to put the time into perspective by counting backward. What was I doing when I was eleven years old, I thought to myself. Shit! I couldn't fucking remember. That was a long ass time ago.

My mother spoke for me at sentencing. She told the judge that I was a father figure to my sisters and mentioned how I had helped raise them. She made sure the court knew I never used a weapon, even though I was carrying out a serious crime in a nonviolent manner. But the judge disregarded her statement and said I was "one of the most violent people to ever enter his courtroom" when issuing my sentence.

He must have just been transferred over from traffic court, I suppose, because I never used a weapon and never so much as farted on my way out of the banks. Never said I'd hurt anyone, and never stopped anyone from leaving. My parents had also raised me to be polite. Most of the tellers interviewed by the Feds had stated that aside from me robbing them, I seemed like a really nice guy. I was the ideal bank robber, in my opinion.

Either way, I got my eight years, my two strikes, and a free bus ride to the Richard J. Donovan Correctional Facility, a state prison near San Diego and not even two miles from the Mexican border.

11
THE FIRST DAY OF SCHOOL

I WAS LUCKY, the way I saw it. The criminal justice system doesn't give a fuck about how young or old you are. They just see a long-term burden literally staring them in the face. With the way our corrections system runs, they're probably right to think that.

If you graph out the amount of growth in the California prison system, it looks like a fucking winning stock. Long-term projections and all, a real money-making operation, and it will stay that way. If nothing changes, that is. So eight little ass years compared to what they would have liked to have given me wasn't looking so bad. I was ready to do that shit.

Screw *Orange Is the New Black*, my first day of prison was real shit. It was gloomy and drizzling as a line of us new prisoners stepped off the bus handcuffed and shackled. Welcome home.

We went through the intake process, which consisted of a gang tattoo check (at that time I had only a nongang-related San Diego Padres logo on my forearm and "In It to Win It" above and below) and a quick explanation of what they expected out of us. I sat in front of a plainclothes officer at a small wooden desk in a small outdated office. In front of him was a file. He opened it and began to read. Another officer walked in, stood next to his chair, and began reading my file as well.

My case was well known in San Diego at the time. Several news cameras had been present for some of our court sessions. While visiting me in county jail after a court appearance, my mom told me that she was overwhelmed at how serious my case actually was. She had said that she didn't understand how the guy being charged with murder that had gone out ahead of me garnered no reaction from the cameras. But as soon as my co-defendants and I stepped in the courtroom, the cameras were at the ready and filming immediately.

The officer seated in the chair began his questioning: "You a gang member?"

"Nope."

He looked back down at my file. "You have two strikes. You can either do your eight years, or do life. Up to you. Go back to the tank." Questioning over.

He was telling me, in so few words, that if I so much as popped somebody, and that person presses charges for assault and battery, even a tiny drop of blood shed, even if the other guy initiated the fight, game over. I would stay there forever.

A couple dozen of us were ushered off to the reception yard in a single-file line by a very demanding guard with a raspy country accent.

We looked up at the gun towers surrounding the yard. Inside, the guards with guns are in a control tower overlooking the cell block. Signs at various places were posted: NO WARNING SHOT. Everyone knew they meant it too. Entering the county jail you hear the stories of prison from people who were regular guests. One thing that becomes clear is that the guards in prison can be trigger happy, according to the stories I had heard anyway.

There were a bunch of homies from various neighborhoods around my age that I quickly made friends with. Two of whom were set to serve a similar amount of time as I was. They had heard of my exploits and were eager to hear my story. I had already been convicted of the crimes, so I had no problem telling them the details. Smurf from Del Sol said it all sounded sick, and that I should write a book. I don't remember what I responded with, but here we are.

A few weeks later I was transferred to the facility-two yard, which was a level-three facility. Prisons have different levels that are based on the security risk of each prisoner. Level one is the lowest security, and level four is the highest general population security level. Max custody status is reserved specifically for people in the SHU (Solitary Housing Unit) or in the hole.

I had already heard that I had a few older homies on that yard. They were actually related to some of my homies from the street and were aware that I'd be coming. Apparently one of them had the right connections and got me over there by pulling some strings.

The prisons were so overcrowded, I was housed in the facilities gym. Row upon row of metal bunk beds, some two high, with most being three high. I landed in the middle of two other bunks. I felt like a fucking canned good stacked on a shelf, but it was home for now.

Bunks and cells are segregated by race or gang affiliation in California prisons, and for good reason. Races cling together for backup and the kind of protection the system can't offer. The groups are typically referred to as cars. You couldn't allow another person from any other car to bunk up or cell up with you at any time—a good rule to avoid getting your throat slit by an enemy as you slept.

Because of my bright whiteness and shaved head, Woods (white, general population inmates) would often approach me and confuse me for one of their own. I'd quickly inform them, "I'm a *Sureno*" (South Sider), letting them know what car I rolled with.

The homies in the car ran a tight ship. Legal paperwork would be checked upon arrival to any new building you landed in (to ensure you didn't have any funny charges such as sex-related offenses). Beds were made and mattresses were rolled up each morning to show discipline. Working out was a must. Shoes would be worn at all times outside of the cell/bunk area or showers.

If you did not yet have shoes, a homie that worked in the yard's laundry would find you some. If one of us jumped (participated) in a riot, everyone present at the time would be expected to join in it. There was no room for cowards or dead weight. You're trained to die for any of the homies in a riot if the situation were to arise—to just dive in with no thoughts of your release date being affected or personal injury that could occur. So a member of the car better be ready to die for you if you were to need him.

On my first day at yard, I strolled around looking for my older homies. The yard was a mixture of loose dust, concrete handball and basketball courts, and a pit with workout bars encompassed by a concrete curb, with scattered patches of short grass and dirt taking up the large majority of the remaining area.

During the rainy seasons, things would pick up, and the clovers would pop up in thick, dark green patches. There were no trees. Not a fucking twig. So I learned to appreciate nature a little more. But for most of the year it was pretty desert-like.

Except when it rained spiders. Tiny little black spiders actually fell on us from the sky. My guess is the spiders get it on up in the gigantic lights that tower above the prison yards and lay thousands of eggs. Then, when they hatch, the tiny little monsters release a small strand of web, catch the wind, and find their new home while floating the wind, like in *Charlotte's Web*. Except in the extended cut, the babies are raining down on us in a prison yard and their new home is my face. Fuck yeah nature. You really know how to pick someone up when they're down.

I eventually found an older brother of two of my friends from the street. I had actually met him once when he had just been released from a short stint in county when I was thirteen. He had been busted shortly thereafter and had already served about five years of a nine-year sentence for burglary.

His name was Sad Boy. His prison term initially started off as a maximum two-year sentence. But because it was a residential burglary, and he had signed for a previous strike before, well shit, they just made it four years for him. But wait, there's more. He got another five years of enhancements for having been to prison before and being a gang member. So where someone new to the system would have probably gotten probation, and a strike, he got nine years. Where's the rehabilitation in that?

He made the best of prison and, at times, seemed like he could really enjoy it. He was more well fed than actually sad, despite his name. That's how I wanted to be, just coasting through time. People lose their damn minds in there stressing on what their girls are doing at home and with whom they're doing it with or how many more years or months they have left on their sentences. Why stress? It's already happening to you. Move on to the next objective.

No one liked a stress case. It brought everyone down and came off offensive to those who didn't have a release date. The lifers, well, those dudes did not want to hear from guys complaining about how they still had five years to go on their GTA sentence, when those dudes still had two hundred years to go on a few murders or, even worse, life for petty theft under the three strikes law, or any other various reasons to get life.

"Check your emotions at the gate" (referring to the entrance of the prison) is what we would tell the stress cases. Someone always has it rougher than you.

I preferred making the best of my situation and asked Sad Boy, "What the fuck do we do for fun?"

"All kinds of shit," he said. "Play handball, work out, play football, work out, go to work, work out."

This motherfucker did not look like he did any form of working out or sport-like activities to me. He then continued, "I just pretty much chill, play handball, and get fucked up."

This guy could have just led off with the getting fucked up part, Jesus Christ. "Get fucked up how, like with what?" I wanted to know.

"With pruno (a prison wine), white lightning (prison liquor)," he said. "Or you can find weed, heroin, and I think there's a guy with coke too."

"Fuck yes, please and thank you, where do I line up?"

He laughed and said, "It all cost money, you got any money left from those hits?"

"Nope, Feds got it," I replied.

"Well then you better get a hustle, little homie."

Well shit, I thought, that's what I do best.

12

HOTEL CALIFORNIA

I WAS TRYING to live life as comfortably as possible. I didn't use many drugs, but I knew if I could get some, I would eat very well and wash that food down with bottled soda when I sold that shit to someone else.

Good thing for me I'm somewhat of an artist. I was doing drawings on envelopes and handkerchiefs in return for shit like coffee, soups, beans, sodas, tortillas, pastries, and various other awesome food items throughout my time in county jail. It turned out a nice drawing on a handkerchief in prison was the equivalent of fifty dollars, as was a quart of prison liquor.

We'd use a razor blade to cut a square about a foot plus two inches from a prison bed sheet. Then fray the edges about two inches by de-threading the sides. In the center, I'd draw using a pen or pencil. The cotton would help with the shading on the drawings.

Lots of guys wanted drawings of girls with boobs hanging out or prison themes. Often prisoners would order a handkerchief for somebody on the street, say a daughter or son, and want a Disney character. Prison art is kind of valuable as art. People even frame them. But for me, it was currency.

I got approached by a Wood one afternoon in my block's dayroom, and he asked if I could do him a handkerchief in exchange for a quart of white lightning. He was a redneck-looking fellow with pale skin and wiry yellow hair. Even though he looked like a tweaked-out banjo instructor, I said I could indeed. He made good shit and was known to keep his word on expected delivery times.

Three days later I was one quart of white lightning richer. As luck also had it, there was an abundance of hard drugs on the yard at the time that I received my liquor.

Drugs were always sold in heftier portions when they were plentiful, but it never stayed plentiful. I arranged a deal with the dude slanging on the yard. We agreed on an exchange of a fat fifty for my quart of lightning. A fat fifty of heroin is a glob of heroin about the size of a match head in a matchbook only a little larger.

We both took our items to the yard at next unlock and made the exchange. All the users pretty much already owed their entire canteen (prison commissary items) for the next couple of weeks, so I knew selling the heroin then would cost me some profits as I'd have to sell at a discount. By this point I also knew that the prison yard's well of drugs, mostly heroin and meth, would dry up in about two weeks. So if I waited about three weeks and made my move before the yard's supply was replenished, I'd get top dollar and sell the heroin for eighty to a hundred.

I waited, and sure enough, that's what I ended up getting. I realized I could do this prison thing no problem, well at least the hustle aspect of it. Now I just needed to make sure I didn't get stabbed for anything.

I took up playing handball to help pass the time on the yard. The courts like everything else were separated by race. You don't play on the wrong court, whether or not one's available. If you do, it could be interpreted as an act of aggression as though you're seizing their court for your car. Either way, it's disrespectful. So you'd wait your turn for the correct court to come up. Then, through process of elimination, you play the victor of each game. You could play one-on-one or a doubles match.

On one particularly hot, dusty afternoon, I challenged an associate to a friendly game. While waiting our turn for a court to open, we heard the loud echo of a crackling alarm that is set off by prison staff to put the yard down. Each prison building and the yard's gun tower has a blue light perched on a metal pole (electrical conduit) above them with a loud speaker near it.

Prison staff carry an alarm on their belts that they press to put the yard down in the event of any type of disruption—from assaults to an inmate not complying with staff orders. Once the alarm is activated to put the yard down, the light above the building flashes and the alarm begins to sound.

The staff then look for what building the alarm was triggered in (by means of the blue flashing light) and start running that direction. Prisoners are expected to get face down and belly down whenever the yard is put down.

We were trained by our car from day one to not get immediately down regardless of there being no warning shots. We were first expected to survey our surroundings and make sure no other homies were being attacked by staff or any other cars. If a guard was beating a homie senseless, we were expected to return the favor. If a riot was taking place at the opposite end of the yard (which measures around 700 feet long by 200 feet wide), we were expected to run over and assist.

If you refuse to get down, the sniper in the tower can shoot you. They'd reserve live ammo for level fours mostly. But their nonlethal rounds of wooden blocks shot at high speed would take you down just as easily.

On this particular occasion of the yard being put down, my associate and I stopped, looked around, and saw, oh fucking shit, the person behind me got his throat slit. It was in fact a homie that was now wearing a freshly tie-dyed red shirt in a sea of blue, white, and gray clothing. None of our car were doing anything or taking any action—other than getting the fuck away from him. I gathered he must have fucked up and been targeted by the homies for whatever reason, so I proceeded to get down on the ground.

He staggered over toward the yard's gun tower with his shirt only getting redder with every clumsy step he took and then fell. A few minutes later the meat wagon (a tan colored 1980s van with no back windows that acted as the ambulance) rolled through the gate and over to the bleeding victim. A couple officers picked him up off the patch of dirt he had fallen on and put him inside the meat wagon to cart him off to the infirmary. I never asked what it was all about or what he did. I just knew I didn't ever want to be that guy—just another pool of yard blood.

A homie from my neighborhood ended up on the yard with me for a parole violation. He was actually the same guy that had notified me of my retirement due to the fact that the wrong guy had been arrested for my robberies. This same guy gave me some of the best advice I had ever received in there.

We were reminiscing on old times one day while waiting for a handball court to open up. We had been on the topic of getting snitched on and he told me, "Homie, you gotta look at yourself as the most solid person on this yard, trust no one you have no reason to, and you'll avoid getting snitched on in here."

I absorb information a little faster when it makes complete sense, and that bit of advice made perfect sense.

I thought I was being careful with whom I trusted on the streets during my robbery spree, but still ended up having no less than three people I knew cooperating with authorities in one form or another to help with my conviction. I knew I couldn't afford to let that happen again. I was still in full hustle mode, two strikes or not.

I knew life in prison was dished out on a regular basis for any new felony conviction, but fuck it, my game was on point (sharp). I wasn't going to be one of those guys that caught life in prison for drugs or fucking anything for that matter. I kept my business to myself and focused on finding homies of a similar mind-set to click up with for hustle-related purposes, and never told anyone shit about what I had going on, unless they were directly involved with it.

13
UNDER THE BRIDGE

A FRIEND WE'LL call Carl pulled some strings and got me moved to a cell in his block. My new cellmate was called the Crossbow Killer by the media, but we homies just liked to call him Huero. One of the homies in that particular block (whom we'll call Gucci) was the homie with the most juice in our car out of the entire institution.

Gucci could have had people killed with just the amount of effort it took to say, "Whack him," and he was a fan of my exploits on the streets. He had read of my robbery spree while doing some time in the SHU (solitary confinement) and found it to be entertaining and impressive. Gucci was a good dude who would often look out for me. He didn't seem to be mad with power or quick to have homies hurt for small violations of our car's rules. He brought a human element and logical manner of thinking into his decision-making, it seemed.

My friend Carl also happened to be close to Gucci as they had already served a few years together by the time I arrived. Carl was a large Hispanic homie. He'd been living very right in his years there, kind of large. He and Gucci always seemed to have everything I wished I had in there: good food, good clothing, drugs galore, and the respect of all the homies throughout our institution. No one really knew too much about their day-to-day business.

You never knew when something, or someone, was going down until it happened, unless you were a member of the right squad. I wanted to have that sense of security in there, but I knew I would need to earn it. I just preferably needed to try and do it in a way that didn't end up with me serving a life sentence. As luck would have it, I seized an opportunity.

I was assigned a job in the prison's main kitchen—a huge area with a tiled, brick red floor and walls made of wood but layered with linoleum or sheet metal. The kitchen contained several different rooms with doors that would remain locked to keep the prisoners that were inside the kitchen from stealing the food products they were working with. Upon exiting any of these rooms, a free staff or correctional officer would pat you down just to make sure you weren't sneaking any goods out. Free staff were state employees hired from outside the prison, thus they were "free."

Several good homies like Creeper from Market Street, Bones and his brother Animal (both from National City), Goblin (resident of El Cajon), Chato from South Los, Villain from Logan Heights, and Trips from South Side Diablos, to name only a few, would help pass the time there.

The kitchen also contained offices for staff members and several large industrial refrigerators that could be up to 60 feet long by 20 feet wide, if I remember correctly, along with a few storage/break areas where pans of various sizes were stored between uses.

The staff offices were almost always locked, unless there was work going on such as restocking, and some were to have no prisoners in them at all unless you were with a staff member. Most refrigerators were also locked, unless being restocked or items were being removed for distribution. Those rooms and refrigerators contained fresh vegetables, meats, cookies, sugar, coffee, ice cream, juice, and just all around good shit.

I knew I needed all of that goodness in my life. I also knew vegetables, meat, and sugar were in high demand on the yard and could fetch a pretty penny.

My first job assignment there was as a cook (I lied and said I had one year cooking experience from the streets), and it worked. My station was at the back of the kitchen in a fairly large open area near two staff offices, which had windows facing the cooking area. There were four or five large bowl-like steam-powered cooking pots about 5 feet wide at the top, with a depth of about 3 feet.

They were all positioned alongside each other with a metal wall directly behind them, which contained the steam and water pipes. Each pot had a red hose next to it that was used for cooking and cleaning purposes. Aside from the two staff offices, the cooking area also contained four large refrigerators and a storage room used mostly for the hot commodity items. The industrial refrigerators were all locked with a chain that connected from the wall to the door's handle. With a padlock finally locking the handle to the short piece of chain bolted to the wall.

Being left alone was a common occurrence in the kitchen no matter where you were stationed. I needed to capitalize on those moments whenever they were presented to me. I began studying everything around trying to find flaws in security or materials I could use to help me get through their security features.

The first thing I realized was the building material itself. The refrigerators and office doors were made of metal. The walls were made of wood and coated with linoleum. The ceiling however, was made of drywall. I could get through drywall, no problem. But it wouldn't be feasible to just bust a hole through a ceiling, then bust another hole in the ceiling of the target location just for some coffee. It would essentially bring down the full wrath of the guards upon the entire kitchen once they realized what had happened.

One day I witnessed a free staff and his inmate laborer go into the ceiling to make some repairs. There were metal hatches on the ceiling that remained locked, which allowed access to the inside. I saw that there was enough room up there to stand easily and a light next to each hatch door inside so workers could see what they were doing. I needed to find a way into that hatch, and therefore the ceiling.

I figured if I could do that, then I may be able to use the hatch as an access point to the ceiling and then drop into the interior rooms that contained the goodies. The locks would prove difficult to bypass with only the small windows of time I would have to myself, so I had to find another way.

I found my way while cooking up some oatmeal one day. The steam from the pots had slightly warped the drywall on the ceiling directly above me. I could get through it easier than I had first thought, but how would I cover the hole so it was undetectable? During the surveillance of my surroundings in the past, I noticed the wall behind our pots had small black screws holding in the thin metal panels, and they were somewhat easy to remove. I also knew pieces of cardboard were abundant in the kitchen.

The kitchen, the cooking pot, and my ceiling gateway to heaven.
Bloomberg/Getty Images

The milk that came in was delivered on blue plastic pallets. The milk itself was in plastic crates. Between the bottom layer of milk and the blue plastic pallet was a sheet of thick white paper. Kind of like the thickness of a greeting card and somewhat close in color to what I was looking for. Glue was always fully stocked in the staff offices, and it wasn't considered an item to have under lock and key. I had just about everything I'd need.

I began making it a point to spray the ceiling near my pot with hot water every chance I had. I sprayed that fucking thing for weeks. Eventually it warped so bad that it was quite obvious it could come down at any point. I told the free staff in charge of our area that we should ask maintenance to fix it before a chunk fell into the food we were cooking. I told him I was heading toward the maintenance office (which was at the opposite end of the kitchen and completely out of sight of the cooking area) and asked if he wanted me to inform them of the needed repair.

He told me to go ahead and let them know. I walked that way but never mentioned it to maintenance. I collected a few pieces of cardboard, snatched up some milk crate paper, stole some glue, acquired four small black screws from the metal paneling behind my pot, and took all my items to an unlocked and unmonitored refrigerator. There I proceeded to make my own piece of "drywall."

The free staff would leave right on cue every day, and the cooks (myself included) would be left behind to finish up the cleaning. It was during one of these times that I meticulously used a small razor blade to remove the piece of warped drywall (approximately 2 feet by 2 feet) and insert my piece in its place. It looked very convincing. So much so that it remained undetected for almost a year.

The cardboard was layered until I had the correct thickness needed and the white paper glued on top in several layers to give a true white drywall look to it. I then compressed it under a tipped-over food cart and let it dry, checking on it often to make sure it didn't get too flat.

Once ready, I inserted the screws at each corner to give the appearance that my piece was screwed in securely. In fact magnets were used to actually attach it to the metal cross sections the real drywall had originally been attached to. I had my access point. The next day our free staff just assumed our work request had been completed.

I needed a spotter during all this and had a homie from my trusted group keeping watch. He had caught his bus ride to prison around the same time as I did and was around my age. He was also a hustler. We began working as a team in the kitchen and stealing whatever we could get our hands on. Our system was so good that we didn't even need to attempt dropping into the secured rooms. We had a stash spot for our items and just needed to find a way to transport it back to our yard.

Carrying veggies, pastries, or meats wasn't an option as we were patted down before leaving work and then finally forced to strip down and walk through a metal detector before reentering the yard. I won't go into detail as to not ruin the hustle for anyone currently exploiting it, but we were using everything the state provided us with to get anything and everything we needed back to our yard, with some outside assistance from people in other critical areas.

This homie and I became the go-to guys for main kitchen goods. We could provide the sugar and juice needed for making pruno in large portions and the hard-to-get vegetables and meats for people to cook with inside their cells.

In case you need the recipe for pruno, here it is. For starters, crush up a bunch of apples or peaches in a plastic bag; keep it warm so it starts to ferment. Add some sugar to keep it going. Now you have your kicker. Four days later, add a gallon of juice with more sugar (two to three pounds depending on the strength of your kicker). Wrap the bag in a blanket or towel and bundle this up under your bed.

After a day or so, the bag will become bloated with gases, so take the ink cartridge out of a Bic pen and insert the plastic tube in the knot of the bag. Tie a string around the bag and tube so the alcohol can breathe (you don't want the bag leaking or exploding). About three days later, enjoy.

Gucci and Carl would regularly put in requests for certain items such as jalapenos, cilantro, bell peppers, tomatoes, and roast beef. I would fill those orders, no problem. I never asked for payment from those two even though they offered it. Instead I would simply tell them not to trip on it and to just hook me up with some of their food or pruno that they made with the ingredients. They seemed happy with this arrangement.

One day a certain person hit the yard who was not in good standing with the car. Carl had mentioned this to me, and I had quickly offered to take care of the situation. He declined and said they already had someone in place to handle it, but was appreciative of my willingness to help.

He told Gucci of what I had offered to do, which somewhat impressed him, and from that point on, I was one of only a few people they would regularly chill with. I was still required to put in work when called upon, but for the most part, I was just chilling.

They not only had trust issues but had grown wary of homies constantly asking for things such as drugs, and then having no money or products to pay for them. Handouts happened, but they were typically reserved for people who had put in work or people who could do some sort of favor later down the line.

Heroin was the drug of choice in there, and it was available frequently. I would see a lot of homies having a good time that seemed carefree of the situation we were all currently in. Being locked up sucked, but they seemed to cope with it just fucking fine, and actually seemed to enjoy it, while on heroin, that is.

I figured giving heroin a try was a good idea. I however didn't want to pay for it, but didn't want to be a beggar either. So I asked Carl for a little bit in return for a hefty order of his choosing from the kitchen.

He didn't have any to give because he was quite fond of using his portions right the fuck up, but suggested I hit up Gucci with the same offer. Gucci used heroin too but also liked to eat well. I never asked him for the deal, but I suppose Carl had mentioned it to him, because Gucci made it a point to find me on the yard. He asked me why I wanted to try heroin and reminded me that I was only nineteen or twenty years old. He also told me that unpaid drug debts were a big reason why people got stabbed in there.

I hate awkward moments. Like this one: One of my first days at chow on the reception yard, I had sat at an available four-seat table with a homie directly across from me, and two clear veteran Woods on both my right and left sides. The homie and I had been talking about the ex-girlfriend I had just prior to my arrest. They were serving fried eggs that day.

I hadn't had one of those in over seven months because when I first came to Donovan, the prison was on lockdown for racial tensions. Our meals were served to us in our cells for weeks. As far as my time in county jail goes, only the finest instant egg mix was served (tasted like cardboard soaked in cooking oil).

The homie across from me had a small bottle of Louisiana hot sauce, a very thin vinegary-type chili sauce, that he had obtained from the canteen (inmate commissary).

I was waiting on him to finish dousing his food so I could have a go. I was in the middle of answering a question the homie had asked me about my ex when he passed me the hot sauce across the table. Hell yeah, spicy fucking deliciousness, here I come.

I began to say, "So this fucking bitch—" when I heard, "HEY, HEY, HEY!" in a loud, startled manner as I shook the bottle of hot sauce in my right hand to raise up all the precious spices sunk at the bottom of it. Only the cap was already off.

I had doused the roughly forty-five-year-old, heavily tattooed, shaved head, handlebar mustache Wood's face with about three good pumps from the quarter-inch opening of the homie's Louisiana hot sauce bottle. I had a wide range of thoughts and feelings at that time, but I mostly just felt awkward. If shit was going to crack off into a riot, so be it. But I'd be the hot sauce guy forever. Fuck.

I looked exactly my age at the time (nineteen). I may as well have fired off a flare in the middle of a chow hall full of people and announced to everyone, "Hi, I'm Richard Stanley, they call me Bandit, I'm new here!" from on top of a table, with a nerdy wave of the hand in the form of chili juice to a not-so-friendly face.

As I looked at the results of my folly, anticipating the worst, the hot-sauce-faced Wood began to laugh. He could see it was an accident and said to me, "Don't even trip on it, kid. Happened to me once too."

The homie across from me had a look of relief on his face. So, yeah, awkward moments suck. And there I was talking with Gucci about heroin.

I told Gucci I just wanted to give it a shot because it seemed to help people cope with their current environment and seemed to make their days go by faster. As they say, time flies when you're having fun, right? At least that's how my teenage mind perceived it.

He just listened and kind of retreated into his own thoughts for a bit. We were walking along the track for a while listening to the music coming from his Super 3 boombox he held by a handle down by his side, and he told me to meet him in his cell at next unlock. He said he would prefer to administer the dose himself to ensure I didn't die. I agreed and was in his cell at next unlock.

Once inside, he took out his stash (about a half ounce of heroin) and broke off a small piece. He put the piece into a spoon and mixed in some hot water. The water broke down the heroin and formed a dark brown soup-like substance that we call *calditos* (soups). He instructed me to lie on the bunk on my back and lean my head over the side so he could pour the mixture into my nose.

I did as instructed while he proceeded to fill my nostril with the substance. It burned horribly. From my nose, straight to the back of my skull. He said to lie like that for about a minute, then sit up. I sat up, began to cough, and told him I didn't feel anything but burning.

He looked somewhat shocked and began to say something when—fuck yes! It hit me, and hit hard. He noticed the change in my eyes and asked, "You feel it now, don't you?" with a smile on his face.

I said, "Hell yes, I feel it," and continued with, "this shit's fucking great!"

He told me not to like it too much and warned me that he'd have to have me handled just like anyone else if I were to become in debt on the yard and be unable to pay for it. I told him he wouldn't need to worry about that. I wouldn't let it happen. We chilled until next unlock, which was "yard recall" when they called everyone in from outside and the dayrooms to lock it up in their cells. This yard recall was to prepare for evening chow.

I exited his cell when his roommate came in, and I returned to my own. I was fucked up beyond anything I had ever experienced to that point. I felt relaxed and in a state of complete euphoria. I was also itchy and very thirsty. I drank a bunch of Tang out of my tan plastic cup and waited for chow time to come around. I nodded out from my high and only snapped out of it when the cell doors began to crack open for chow.

I still felt extremely high but managed to walk my ass to the chow hall. I'd have to make the roughly 200-foot walk there, then dodge the two or three cops at the chow hall door, and then make it past another on my way out after I finished eating. Simple enough. I figured I could do it, no problem.

I made it in and past the cops just fine, but had several homies taking notice of my highness. They began asking me if I had more, or if I could get more. I didn't mention who gave it to me, just said I was hooked up with a small portion by a homie. I couldn't eat much so I just had some of the corn that was included on my tray.

I started to feel like I needed to vomit and felt it coming on strong. As I emptied my tray and returned it to the scullery window, I turned and began walking to the exit door when my stomach surged. I held it in, but just as I was walking past the cop at the exit, corn and Tang came shooting out my nose.

I ran over to a patch of dirt outside the chow hall and let it all out. The officer called me over and asked me if I was all right. I told him I was fine and that the medical officer had diagnosed me with possibly having the stomach flu earlier in the day, and if god wills it, I should be fine. Thankfully he took my word for it and let me go.

Even considering the technical difficulty I experienced at the chow hall, I still found heroin to be completely awesome at the time. That day flew by for me. Now I needed to make the next five or six years go by just as fast, but also continue to eat well.

I had to grow my hustle so I could afford my new lifestyle. I was definitely not going to become a fiend or let myself get in debt. I had heard rumors on the yard about cell phones being available for the right price. If I had one of those, I could get things moving right along, but trying to bribe an officer was a crime. I would need to take my time on that project and do it right or risk a lengthier sentence. Asking Gucci wasn't an option, in my opinion. It would probably put him on edge having someone asking about his business and connections.

Carl however was my homeboy, and I would have better luck asking him, I thought. When I asked Carl, he said, "You got a thousand dollars? 'Cause that's what the cops are charging."

I reminded him that he already knew I did not have that kind of money, but told him if I had a cell phone I could make things happen, I was sure of it. Typically when someone goes to prison for a lengthy term, their friends and girls fall off within the first two years. Out of sight, out of mind. I had yet to hit that obstacle. I had fresh resources on the streets and hadn't lost contact with all of them, and some owed me favors. He didn't give me any other leads, but I knew I needed to get a cop on the team.

Having a cell phone was only a contraband write-up in prison at the time. Even so, if you had one, you weren't telling anyone. If you were found in possession of a cell, it was thirty days added on your sentence that you could in turn get back if you were disciplinary-free for ninety days and a short stay in the hole—usually two weeks to a month. Shit, I could do that.

I started listening to every conversation the cops would have among themselves in hopes of hearing any sign of financial distress at home or discontent with their employers. It took me just over two years, working on the same cop the entire time before that cop finally cracked. Interesting how someone's drinking problem can make them so vulnerable. So who's the criminal here? Well, both, I guess.

There will be no details of how I accomplished this or who this person was, but they were very loyal to me and knew I was too. Prison snitches fail to realize that cops have access to their confidential files. Cops also talk to one another about their confidential informants out on the yard and the type of information they provide. I would have to assume this is a good way for cops knowing who to fuck with and who not to fuck with.

So, thank you, prison rats. Because of how many of you there are out there, and the systems that were put in place by the cops to manage your shit information, combined with your lack of loyalty and integrity, you made it easier for the cop to trust me. See, snitches, no matter what anyone says, you're not "completely" worthless, just mostly. And what did prison rats get in return? Maybe a radio or TV or food.

Gucci and Carl fell victim to prison rats and were put in solitary confinement. Carl was eventually transferred to a level-four yard at a different facility, and Gucci was validated as a prison gang leader and sent to spend the remainder of his time and any time he may catch thereafter in a solitary housing unit, under an indeterminate SHU. Meaning, there was no guaranteed release from the SHU or placement back in the general prison population—ever.

You're deemed a threat to the safety and security of the entire institution, thrown in the darkest hole the state has to offer, and forgotten about. By then I had already heard stories of people being in the SHU for over fifteen years with no end in sight. How that's not torture, I'll never understand, but those types of sentences were dished out often by our captors whenever you'd get under their skin enough.

The SHU is different from the hole, believe me, I know. The SHU is where you go forever, while the hole is hell where you go for what seems like forever. Like a prison sentence within a prison sentence, inmates sent to the SHU get some comforts such as radio and TV, but they're going to be there for a while, alone, in a cell.

The process of validating someone (determining if you are a prison gang member) in the California prison system is a joke, and I'll dive deeper into this later, trust me. But for now, let me tell you that the committees in charge of dishing out these unending SHU terms were heavily influenced by the same people who first put in the paperwork to have it done (typically the investigative services unit or ISU).

As a prisoner, you are allowed an appeals process, but guess who has to help you do the appeal and investigation into your case? An officer assigned by the people on the committee. I suppose calling it a joke is somewhat of an understatement. I'd call it *criminal*, which is far more suitable a description in my opinion.

The ISU or Gooners were the cops who pursued such cases as inmates with cell phones and officers smuggling in contraband among various other things. The ISU are very similar to prison snitches in a way. They have no loyalty to their own and are just in it for the benefits. These guys were known to be foul and quick to step outside the law—when the cameras were off.

For example, they'd been known to plant drugs and organize gladiator fights between prisoners up in Corcoran, another state prison, where inmates fought to the death. They would release two separate cells in a solitary building. Each cell containing a rival member of the other. You either fight. Or you die. Sometimes the guards just shot them afterward anyway.

Think I'm full of shit? Google it. But now why hasn't anyone heard of that? The same way no one heard about my thirteen-year-old self being harassed by police for no reason, but with plenty of spectators to see. Because only the cop's word counted.

Shit may be starting to change on the streets now with cell phone cameras, but in prison, it's just your word against theirs. So long story short, you didn't fuck with these guys too hard because you knew they fought dirty, and their words beat yours in court.

As you can see, I still maintain a certain a level of contempt for these ISU officers. These guys wouldn't have a job if it wasn't for prison snitches, so they were only going to catch me if I was loose with my words. No worries there. Plus I learned how to navigate a few other obstacles at work and gained access to the freezers that were used for storing the good shit.

With my new phone, I now had access to my resources on the street and all the hot-ticket food items anyone could want, plus I built up a canned food and sugar supply in my ceiling stash. I could always fall back on that and be all right.

14

TRYING TO FLOAT THROUGH TIME

ONCE YOU FIND a cellmate that you can trust and get along with, you develop a friendship and firm sense of loyalty with that person. I had to be selective about who was living in the cell with me. You can't really hide things such as cell phones and a PlayStation with your cellmate only a few feet away. So being picky was extremely critical. If a guy moved out, I would already have someone in mind to take his place. It would be done as soon as possible to avoid a random person being placed in my cell by staff.

Sometimes finding a trusted replacement wasn't all that easy, because no one wanted to abandon their current cellmate. For the most part I avoided random people from falling in with me, but occasionally one would slip in temporarily, and I'd have to put business on hold till I could get them out. Whoever ended up living with me was very lucky in one way, but so very unlucky in other ways.

Two guys would live in very cramped space with metal lockers, upper and lower bunks, a desk and metal stool for the desk all welded to the concrete walls or floor.

On the outside wall, we had a vertical window about five inches wide and three feet tall.

Our lockers held our clothing such as sweat pants, shorts, sweaters, and thermals in the high-fashion colors of gray or white only; legal paperwork; and other property—we were allowed six cubic feet of property. Think about it. We also were allowed a TV and a fan or radio (in the desert, you want a fan). And electrical outlets were available, of course. Hot pots were available; we had them for boiling water and cooking meat and other food.

The décor was grungy, everything was grungy with concrete cracks and rusting rebar, but our sinks were shiny as hell. The metal sinks didn't come that way, but we used sandpaper from the wood shop to shine them up. That dark square on the wall above the sink used to be a mirror. Now the sink became our mirror.

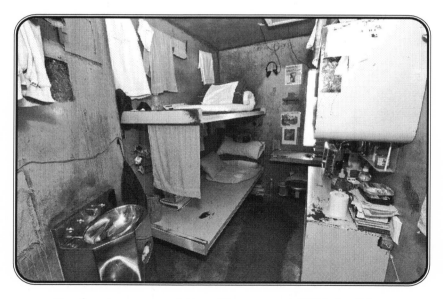

Our five-star accommodations. Photo courtesy KPBS, San Diego.

Hispanics in my car rolled up their mattresses on the metal bunks. You didn't want to be lying on your sheets because they'd get dirty from our clothes, the yard, and desert dust. With mattresses rolled, we signaled we were not lazy. It also meant we were ready for the doors to crack if the guards were in need of entertainment with a gladiator fight. The control booth guard could flip a switch and pop the door to the cell at any time.

Some guys would wax their concrete floors to a high shine and wax in images of naked girls or team logos.

The bottom bunk is preferable, but in our car if you have a medical disability or are over a certain age, you get the bottom bunk, and the young guy goes up top.

My cell was home, and I found ingenious ways to stash my shit. I wonder if anybody has ever found some of my hiding spots to this day. I'd never tell.

One reason to avoid telling people your business in there, besides getting snitched on, is because of the careless people around. These people that I mention would do such things as sit in the dayroom and just stare at my cell, waiting for me to come out, so they could hopefully get a free kick down of some good shit. Often they would walk right up to my cell and try to talk me into just handing something out the side of the cell door. After they had already been warned. The guards would take notice of such things easily. All they had to do was watch.

The drug fiends knew we weren't just allowed to linger by cells during dayroom or yard hours, but would give almost zero fucks. The representatives for our car would often try their best to keep people away from critical doors, usually with either a verbal warning or maybe some burpees (a vigorous squat thrust exercise). Other times it could be a beating. It just depended on if you had already been warned or not.

Nobody wanted the officers or ISU to raid their cell in search of contraband, so nobody wanted unwanted traffic at their doors.

I was one of the two main suppliers of our entire institution and damn near no one but the haters would want me gone anytime soon. Fiends were the biggest culprits. The careless individuals either didn't have the sense to realize they were bringing heat, or didn't care. One is just as bad as the other. I did my best to avoid situations like those I describe, but it would still happen from time to time. I looked out for the right people in there (as one is expected to do) to have the full support of our car's hierarchy, and I did.

Some of the elite members of our car were the same people I had come up to prison with. We already had existing friendships before their promotions, or my hustle, and would hang with each other on the yard frequently. This circle we created was tightly knit. We could talk openly of our business as mine directly affected and benefited theirs. But theirs affected and benefited mine too.

If someone was going to get stabbed or removed forcibly from the yard, I would be told to avoid having anything critical on me during a certain time, and in return I helped keep their business thriving with my connection. We all had something to lose, and we all had something to gain by keeping our talks only between us. It was a perfect system.

Camera phones weren't really a thing when I was out. The first one I owned or saw was in prison. With the help of one of my political friends, we were able to get a mobile phone into every block on our yard. Each block is a separate building entirely, so communication during lockdowns or count times was basically impossible, until we came along. We would send pictures of the drugs we were doing or the video games we were playing to each other during lockdowns. We had that yard sewn up (under control).

The smell of freshly cooked carne asada would often fill the air on the tier at night. Sometimes we'd hook up three or more hot pots with extension cords. By the time the guards smelled the aroma and came searching for the food, it had been eaten and the evidence disappeared.

I would get so high on mixtures of heroin, cocaine, and alcohol that I created my own saying within our circle, "If you ain't barely breathing, you ain't doing it right." A stupid way of thinking I'll admit now, but back then I was just trying to float through time, unbothered.

I even had a pet parakeet at one time. One of those dime-store yellow-and-green parakeets landed on the chain link fence outside while we were walking back from chow. An Asian guy snatched him up, but I paid him a hundred dollars in food items.

I was hardly the Birdman of Alcatraz; my little bird died three days later. I had him bedded down for the night in a shoebox. The joke was that the bird died in the SHU. The Native Americans took the body and created an art plaque from the skull and wings.

Over time I began getting more and more regular visits from the members of the ISU—with surprise 4:00 a.m. searches. They could never catch me with anything, it seemed. I only knew how stressed they really were when they began with the threats of false charges if I kept "pushing it" or the physical harm that may fall upon me.

Physical harm was always a fear. While I was briefly working in the facility-two culinary back in maybe 2003 or 2004, the yard was put down. It looked like all guards were running toward the administrative segregation building (building seven). I was in the chow hall at the time, and all officers previously inside with us had left in response to the alarm. It was just as chow was wrapping up, and there weren't many people left besides the workers. The officer in charge of the chow hall and its workers, whom we'll call Mealworm, had also responded.

We stood up and looked out some of the chow hall's row of windows to see what was happening in building seven. They had pinned down one guy in the clover patch near the concrete bench in front of building eight. A member of the ISU was all over this guy along with about five or six of his friends in green. I was too far away to see punches through the taller than usual clover patch as the guards were mostly all low to the ground, but what I did see next shocked the fuck out of me.

A guard was barely arriving to the scene, somewhat winded, it seemed. He jogged the last few feet there and suddenly dropped his knee on the back of the prisoner's neck. All struggling stopped. The officers seemed to back off. Some began shaking the now motionless black inmate.

The meat wagon showed up, and they put the man on a stretcher. The guy's arms were hanging to the sides with no movement unless it was due to a bounce in step by the now caring and very attentive officers who had placed him on the gurney, and who were now loading him in the back of the makeshift ambulance. Welcome to your own death, kids.

We later received word that the guy had died. Crushed windpipe or broken neck, we were told. To top it off, word was he was having a seizure and not actually resisting. In the next few days there was a homicide detective roaming around for a bit, and then he was gone. An internal agency had been placed in charge of gathering information for the homicide detective's case—the good ol' members of the ISU to be exact. Now I can't comment on their entire investigation, but I can tell you about my personal experience.

A member of the ISU (a tall Russian-looking fucker) was assigned to collect firsthand accounts from inmates who may have seen anything. We were locked down for this part of the investigation and called out of our cells and down to a dayroom table where an ISU officer was waiting. The officer had a handheld recorder that was meant to officially record our statements, I'm assuming.

Once I was called to the dayroom for my turn, the ISU officer turned on his recorder, said his name and that he would be taking my statement, and proceeded to have me recite my own last name and prison number—T-83401—as he placed the recorder on the metal tabletop.

His first question to me was something like, "Did you see the incident that took place on this date at this time?"

"Yes."

"Where were you when you saw this?"

"In the chow hall looking out the window."

He stopped the tape immediately, told me we were done, and instructed me to go back to my cell.

A couple years later I read an article that said one of the guards had been found responsible to some degree in civil court for the inmate's death, with a brief mention of a few other officers. The family of the man had been awarded some cash, but that's all I saw in the short article.

Apparently no one told the guard he was a killer, or fired him for the workplace violence thing, because he was still there, bothering me and my new circle. I had left the article on my desk with his name highlighted in it for the ISU to find on their next search. I left it there every day until it happened.

They were only in my cell for around five minutes (very short period of time for an ISU search) that time. Nothing was really missing but an article that time. It was perfect. They knew it was a touchy issue. No one had lost their job for the death of the inmate, and it was one hot tip away from being news. Too bad it was just another inmate dying on another yard, in whatever the fuck prison. Because no hot tip ever came.

About a year before my release, our old friend the bad guard of the ISU and the star of our officer-related inmate death story ended up killing another inmate. A young homie from North County San Diego lost his life in the facility-one visiting room, in front of his niece and various other visitors of inmates. Guards believed the homie was smuggling in narcotics. And the inmate ended up dead at the end of it, laced in mace.

He was found to be in possession of marijuana. His sentence was already carried out for the violation though. The sentence of death. Good thing that guard was there to do some protecting and serving again, or the inmate may have smoked that weed and ate a bunch of snacks all night. Conveniently the cameras were down that day so the guard again kept his job.

If an inmate has two strikes and one of these human being officers, with their human emotions and flaws, just says "that inmate hit me!" well shit, that inmate might just get life in prison, despite the circumstances of what initiated it. Even if the guard is the aggressor. What if they had waited until the homie had exited the visiting room to approach him? Or what if he had fought back a little harder, a little quicker, and survived his assault, would he have gotten life in prison for battery on a peace officer? It's possible if he had two strikes. But that's just the way it is.

Early one afternoon I was lying on my bunk watching TV during a surprise lockdown. I had a small bundle of marijuana that was tied up in plastic clutched in my hand. My door began to open before the ISU came running up the metal stairs in their dumb-ass green jumpsuits, keys fucking jangling. I had an obstructed view and threw the bundle of weed into my mouth and reached for a nearby cup of peach drink I had, but heard, "DON'T FUCKING MOVE, STANLEY!" before I could grasp the cup.

I proceeded to swallow my bundle (or try to anyway), wishing I had that drink in my hand, when the shit gets lodged in my throat. They're stripping out my cellmate first while one officer keeps his eyes solely on me and my every move. I'm fucking choking to death and trying to keep my composure and not give off an "I'm choking on drugs" kind of vibe while this is all happening.

Now it was my turn. They instruct me to take off my clothes, lift up my arms, turn around, lift up my feet, bend at the waist and cough twice, all while this weed slowly lurches down my throat, still obstructing air. Once I'm turned around and upright, the officer instructs me to open my mouth. I did as ordered, and as I did, the package slipped down my throat and was never detected by the officer.

I put my boxers back on, was put in handcuffs, and then escorted to the dayroom benches in the TV area. A US Customs agent and his K-9, accompanied by a member of the ISU, were headed in the building and to my cell. I was then approached by a different member of the ISU and escorted outside the building.

When exiting the building, I realized what was happening as I was being led to sit on the concrete handball courts. They were targeting everyone they believed to be selling drugs or considered a heavy hitter, all cars included.

There were about four US Customs K-9 units, and they were taking the drug-sniffing dogs into every building and cell they thought may contain the big stash. With all their efforts, they couldn't find shit on me.

At next yard my circle and I grumbled over the search and complained of the items the ISU had confiscated during the hit when they couldn't find what they originally hoped for. As one of my associates passed me a joint, and I a cup of lightning to him, he got a phone call. He had an earpiece and would regularly walk the yard with us and take calls. It looked as though he was listening to his pocket radio and just talking to us as we walked.

This call was about our next delivery of some coke that was supposed to be good shit. We were under a lot of heat, but everything seemed to be under control. We all had cellphones where a cellphone was needed. If the ISU ran up in a building, we would get an alert from someone inside that building giving us the needed time to get rid of our items. How these items disappeared will have to remain a secret, but we had our ways, and they were effective.

I was making good money. Enough to keep my connection content, my stomach well fed, and enough cash stacked to keep things rolling at a steady pace.

15
SO MANY TEARS

I BEGAN COOKING pruno at work in my ceiling stash spot to avoid the risk of transporting lightning to work for break-time enjoyment. We had two five-gallon jugs going at any given time up there. One prepared two days after the first was started, to maintain a good flow.

The temperature in the kitchen ceiling was perfect for the making of pruno. Nice and hot at all times, no need to babysit it. Just add juice, yeast from the prison bakery, and enough sugar (two to three pounds per gallon of juice), and you were getting fucked up in about three days.

My kitchen crime partner whom we'll call Falls would keep point while I made my way into the hot-ass ceiling through my false piece of drywall. I personally liked to chill my pruno overnight in the cooler when possible. That shit was bomb (highly enjoyable).

We had a new worker that was in the Other car. The Others are a group of prisoners that consisted of anyone who claimed any nationality other than Mexican, white, or black. This guy was tall, black, and spoke with a foreign accent. He had a few months before his release on a GTA (grand theft auto) offense. He was somewhat odd and would frequently just roam the kitchen during his downtime. If he had stumbled upon us while entering the ceiling, it could put our spot in jeopardy.

We approached him and managed to convince him to do us a favor and stay clear of our area at certain times due to

Sureno business taking place. He accepted it and steered clear whenever he was asked to do the favor. He lived in my building and had an Asian cellmate who was serving life, for what I can't recall. They both seemed pretty chill as far as I could tell, but regardless of how they seemed, we didn't want anyone knowing of our stash spot.

Anytime a batch was ready, we looked out for certain people who worked with us, even leaving some stashed in the refrigerators for the arrival of the next shift of workers. We made it so those around us were happy as well. Never having to want something, and not being able to get it because of lack of resources, but never knowing where it was being stashed.

Sugar had been removed from the prison menu due to inmate alcohol abuse. We had the last supply on lock. Hundreds of pounds of sugar sitting in our kitchen's ceiling. We had a Wood place a large order of fifty pounds of pure granulated goodness back on the yard. He said he'd get us three quarts of lightning if we came through and if his batch didn't get busted. We agreed and had him fifty pounds of sugar at his cell door the following day with service better than FedEx.

I couldn't wait for my quart and a half. They sold Tang in the prison packages and orange drink in the yard's store. I'd mix my orange drink with my lightning and have myself a prison screwdriver while out for strolls on the yard.

Cooking one quart of lightning usually took all night, but first you needed the pruno done, which took a few days on its own. My circle and I had planned on making deep-fried burritos to bring out to the yard on the day the lightning was scheduled to be ready. Combined with our J-win boom boxes, coke, and some weed, we'd have a pretty good time. We had three days to go till then.

During nighttime count, two days prior to us getting our alcohol, I noticed a commotion on the other side of my building. Everyone was locked up for the night, so the only people out of cells were cops. I couldn't make out what they were talking about, and it didn't seem to pertain to me so I stashed all my shit just to be on the safe side and crashed out for the night.

The next morning I realized we were on lockdown when the doors didn't open for chow. No prisoners were being let out of their cells for anything. I couldn't get any info about what the fuck was happening, and therefore had nothing to relay to the other buildings. We all decided to put away and keep away our stashes until we got more information. No one wanted to be the guy to get caught slipping (off guard).

The following day they began allowing restricted inmate movement, workers mostly. A guy came to my cell after being released for work, and he lived on that side of the building. He told me an Other had raped and killed his cellmate, rolled him up in bed sheets, and placed his body under the bottom bunk tucked behind some paper bags of food items.

It was in fact my coworker who had three months to release. It wasn't him that was rolled up in sheets now, but him that did the rolling. Three months to home, he rapes and kills his lifer cellmate.

Jesus Christ, now I really needed a drink. I sent word to the lightning cook (also in my building) and asked him to send me over a tumbler of that shit as soon as it was ready. Fortunately we were off lockdown in no time (as it was an isolated incident), and I got to drink the lightning on the yard with my circle. We did blow, smoked weed, and got drunk while listening to some 2Pac Falls had thrown in the boombox and plotted our next moves.

I informed my circle that I had a committee hearing soon and that my points should be dropping to level two. This meant I could qualify to be housed on the prison's minimum yard and not have an electric fence between me and the outside world. I would be able to get a cell phone over there quick and establish communication between the yards if I were to be approved.

I talked to someone in a critical area and asked him to do what he could in exchange for me forming a working relationship with him. I promised to help establish him as a main tobacco connect on the level-three yard with my resources on the minimum yard.

I'd keep the tobacco (loose tobacco like Bugler that came in tins for rolling your own cigarettes) coming until we reached an agreed amount, and then work out a deal from that point on. He told me he would do what he could, so we shook on it and waited for that time to come.

In prison you can deal with extremely manipulative people. Every type of hustler exists in that environment. In turn, you get a wide range of people trying to manipulate you. Given enough time you learn a lot of the game (hustle) that people try and hit you with. I felt I was good at reading people and had always been wary of anyone who regularly tried to include himself in our conversations.

One guy, a real lame, would walk up, midstory, say what's up, and stand there. Just like that. Eventually he'd leave either by being asked to or because of the silence that would fall upon his arrival. He had a small role on the yard and would get weed often, but hadn't been locked up with us that long. He was trying to do too much too soon.

He was a fairly new transfer from Ironwood State Prison and seemed to be desperate to include himself in a heavy-hitting circle, which I found to be odd. We'll call him PC Barbie. Some of the people between us had almost unlimited power on our yard. If I was the new guy on a yard, I wouldn't want to piss those kinds of guys off, and I definitely wouldn't want them to consider me a nuisance, like he was doing.

My suspicions were justified early one evening when I was making a phone call from my cell, sitting on the bottom bunk, watching TV with the lights turned off. An officer approached and turned his back to me to signal the control tower to open my door. I had no time to stash anything. I put the phone in my back pocket while he wasn't looking and calmly approached the door when it was open. I asked what was going on, and he responded, "I don't know, they just asked me to get you out of the cell."

He instructed my cellmate and me to sit in the dayroom and await further instructions. We did as asked and headed down to the benches while the officer proceeded to enter our cell. As soon as we approached the benches, the yard's alarm sounded. I got as close to the cop's office as I could before getting completely down. I was within arm's reach of their office door. The officer that had entered my cell looked confused about what his next action should be.

He talked in his radio, but seemed to get no response. He turned and went back in the cell, to look for contraband, I imagine. He and his partner would often joke with me and tell me that they received my Verizon bill in the mail upon my returning from work or the yard.

"I got T-Mobile," I'd fire back.

So they knew what was up, they just weren't able to catch me. The tower guard, with automatic rifle in hand, was watching me. She eventually turned and looked at the other side of the building allowing me the chance to turn off my phone and hide it inside and behind the cops' office door. It was sitting between the space of the door and the wall behind it. I scooted away from the office and a little closer to the benches.

I knew the cops' office was the last place these fuckers would look for my contraband, but also knew it was better there than on me if a storm of ISU officers were to come rolling in. My cellmate gave me an approving nod and under a whisper asked if I'd grabbed the drug stash.

What the actual fuck? "You had it last!" I told him.

"I think I left it on the table" (referring to the small metal table welded into the wall at the back of each cell), he said.

"What the fuck?" I responded.

Prisons took most medical emergencies seriously, to some degree anyway. Having chest pains was one of those that garnered special attention. My cellmate was in his thirties with his hair already turning gray, I was now twenty-three. Whenever someone had a medical emergency, it was referred to as "man down."

I told my cellmate to go man down. That should force the officer out of our cell and possibly give one of us a chance to dart past him and back into the cell. A fucking good plan in my opinion. I'd rather get thirty days for disobeying a direct order than life for possession. He too was a two-striker and agreed it may work, but refused the plan. He was scared. What the fuck?

"Just say you have chest pains, I'll do the rest," I stated.

He again refused. I told him I was going to go man down and that he in turn needed to do the dashing to the cell and flushing of the drugs. He agreed.

My twenty-three-year-old self rolled onto my back, grabbed my chest, and acted as though I couldn't breathe.

My cellmate began yelling, "MAN DOWN! MAN DOWN!"

The tower officer came over to the side I was on, looked down at me, over at my cell, back to me, then back to the cell, in a calm but confused manner.

She then yelled, "Garcia" (the officer in my cell).

He stepped out of the cell without looking at us first and asked her, "What?"

"This motherfucker's trying to go man down," she quipped.

I continued my show, dying with every second that went on, at least that's how I'd like to think it looked. Garcia stepped toward the metal stairs directly in front of my cell doors and stopped. He was blocking the stairway.

He looked on as I lay there, grasping at my chest, probably thinking I was full of shit, but also knowing how serious this matter was taken. He then instructed my cellmate to get back inside the cell. My cellmate listened and continued up the stairs and stepped inside as ordered. Garcia headed down the stairs toward me while the cell door began closing behind my cowardly and soon to be ex friend.

The tower officer received a call. Then the door began to open again.

"Get him out of the cell, Garcia," she yelled out of the gun tower.

I heard a flush come from the cell and knew the mission was completed either way. Luckily it played out like that or this fool may not have done his part in running up to flush it. I was prepared to do that as well if needed, but was thankful it didn't come to that.

Garcia ran back up and proceeded to have my cellmate strip down. Then in came the ISU. I didn't care, I was looking good on my end. Nothing on me or in my possession. No dope. No phone. They carted me off to the infirmary with an ISU escort.

After a short, awkward ride, we arrived. I was still needing to act as though I was dying while being monitored the entire time by my small audience of guards. They looked confused the whole time. So I take it as a victory regarding my acting skills.

Once I arrived at the prison's central infirmary, there next to me lay this freshly beaten friend of mine on the other side of a Plexiglas window. I looked at him and motioned by throwing up my hands that were cuffed to the gurney now and nodding my head upward with a confused look on my face to signify "what happened?"

Then he tried to tell me.

The ISU had planned a surprise hit just before night yard release. They hit a homie's cell in the next block, and he was also in the process of making a call. His officers entered the cell with him still in it, and he proceeded to flush his phone, or attempt to at least, and injured a female officer's pinky finger in the process.

They fucked this guy up pretty badly. Cuffing him and dragging him down the metal grated stairs and into the sally port where they continued his education on their proper meat tenderizing techniques.

He motioned back with a fist toward his swollen face and pointed at the ISU officer that was at the foot of his bed and looking the other way. He filled me in on his story over fifteen months later when we were housed in the same solitary unit where he had been since I last saw him in the infirmary that night.

Turns out I was all fucked up and dehydrated. You know, from the drugs. They hooked me up to some IVs. I sucked down about two bags of saline, and they cut me loose a few hours later with a clean bill of health. They did an extensive search of my cell but never noticed the phone in their own office.

When I returned to my building, I noticed the cops' office was vacant, and they were watching the television on our side of the dayroom. I knelt down near their office to act as though I was tying my shoe and felt for the phone. Still there! I grabbed it, placed it in my back pocket, and continued toward my cell.

I made it in the pad and asked my cellmate what he had heard, if anything. He said PC Barbie had been busted with weed and snitched everyone out that he believed to be involved in anything at all. I proceeded to immediately gather my items together and get them out of my freshly searched cell, just in case. I informed my cellmate of what happened to our neighbor and reminded him they may have realized their error in letting him back in the cell and may come hit us again.

I took everything out at next unlock and passed it on down the line. I was completely right to do so. The ISU came running up in my cell only a few hours later, this time with one of the main goons, a lieutenant. They placed my cellmate and me in handcuffs and seated us at a dayroom table. I couldn't help but display my happiness at the fact I had beat them again and began laughing and smiling while joking with my cellmate at their pointless attempts to bust us.

The lieutenant didn't like this. He was tall and well over four hundred pounds. I may be way off because he was too big for an officer's uniform. It was a miracle he could even walk. But he walked all of his grouchy ass down the stairs while his beady fucking eyes stayed locked on me.

He approached and stood next to me thrusting his stomach into my shoulder and said, "You wanna keep smiling? How 'bout I come back with a little heroin and 'find' it in your cell, how 'bout that?"

I told him this was unnecessary and that my cellmate had just farted loudly, I meant no offense with the smiling. He didn't buy it but didn't seem to know what else to say in regard to my denial and apology, so he continued back up to my cell and amazingly made it without having an actual heart attack.

Around a half hour later they left empty handed. We entered the cell and began the usual cleanup process after an ISU visit. The ISU isn't all that bad though. They once found pruno cooking in my neighbor's cell and instead of the officer giving him a rules violation that carried four extra months, she just poured it all over his bed, clothing, paperwork, and family photos.

He was already serving life for burglary, so thank god he didn't get those four extra months. I don't know what family photos ever did to that little lesbian chick, but I kept my shit wrapped in plastic after that, and on the top locker—far away from her little hateful heart and hands. Wherever you are, living or dead, I'd just like to say, fuck you, too, bitch.

16
GANGSTAS DON'T LIVE THAT LONG

I'D BE HEADING to the minimum yard soon if I could manage to stay a few steps ahead of my oppressors. I began lining things up so certain people could keep things going smoothly on the yard in my absence.

It was almost perfect timing for me to be transferred to another yard. The ISU was too damn fixated on me. I figured if I were to transfer, the heat and Gooners would follow me, leaving the homies on the level three a little room to breathe and the chance to possibly expand the hustle. I put the right people up on full game (explained in detail) and moved on to my next order of business, making money.

Even though I was doing all right on my end, I still wasn't much of a saver. My main concern was living right. I didn't have the needed discipline to save any large amount of cash for parole purposes. I kept enough saved to fund up to three deliveries, and some for a bribe, just in case. I didn't dip into this fund, and the first profits I made would go right back into the pot for future shipments. I knew making shit happen would be easier on the minimum, but that just meant more opportunity.

If it was as live as I had heard it was, I'd be needing more money. I knew the Gooners would be on my ass over there in a heartbeat too. I figured I'd need to make some bigger moves quickly once I arrived at minimum, before the ISU could fuck it up for me.

I had big plans for establishing a network between prisons. There was an existing one in place but there was too much of a delay, in my opinion. I had a way to distribute resources to three other facilities, but needed a quick way of letting them know when something was on the way. With no heads-up, the package could be intercepted by the guards, or another car. If I could perfect this concept, I'd be making stupid money, six figures a year.

For all that to work I would just need about three extra cell phones, and I'd need to touch bases with the right people at the other institutions. As far as I was aware, there was no system like this in place, nor had there been during my years at the facility. I assumed if I could pioneer that strategy, I may be able to save up a considerable amount of money to make things easier upon my release. A lot easier.

I sent word to the other facilities with homies that were being transferred. But I'd have to wait to hear back from them before I could piece anything else together for the project. I spent the next few weeks as I had the last few years, staying on my toes (aware of my surroundings), getting high, and making money.

I became eligible for a transfer out of level three on a point system. Because I was not there on a sex crime, was not an arsonist, was not validated as a prison gang member, and had less than five years to go, I could be considered.

Once I was dropping down to a level two, I requested to be sent to northern California to go to fire camp. When you see guys fighting the wildfires and they're wearing orange or lime green, these are usually specially trained inmates. My request was denied because they said my case had received too much media attention. I was sent to the level-two building instead.

Soon before my transfer to the minimum, I received word from the main kitchen that the ISU had found the ceiling stash. They brought down about two pallets worth of goods including a couple hundred pounds of remaining sugar. My alcohol hustle had come to an abrupt end. It stung a little, but I was close to being transferred anyway. Whoever snitched out the ceiling spot had cost me about five hundred bucks a month, and probably only gained a few extra packs of cookies doing so. Fucking bottom feeders.

Time came for me to head over to the minimum yard. I hadn't yet received word from the other institutions, so I left instructions with the right person on the level three on how to proceed when they did. I was leaving him my cell phone and told him I'd shoot him a text when I got another one lined up. I wrote down a code and gave him a copy. I'd use that code when initially sending the message so he'd know with certainty that it was me doing the texting and not a guard. He gave me his own code for his response to ensure the same.

My day arrived and I was leaving the yard in better shape than I had found it. I was psyched to find out what kind of shit the homies had going on the minimum. Land of milk and honey, here I come, baby.

Officers escorted me out of the prison gates in a white van with my destination being the minimum yard, no cuffs or shackles. I still had just under three years to go and couldn't help but think about how free I felt and how escaping upon arrival would be so easy. Just a thought was all.

After I went through the yard's intake process, I was approached by several homies that had heard of me and the fact I was known to hang with political figures on the level three. I was somewhat amazed by what I saw around me: almost unrestricted movement, no cells, trees on the yard, no razor wire, and very loose politics.

They wanted to know if I came with any word on political matters (in other words, prison politics). I said no. "I'm just here to chill with the homies a little more comfortably" was my response.

I linked up with a homie who had been on the level-three yard with me a few months prior. He ended up being a rat, so I won't give him the satisfaction of a backstory, but I had given him the job of scoping out the scene and asked him to look for the who's who and the potential hows. He gave me the rundown that the homies had nothing. Only the other cars had items like cell phones.

I had left everything back on the level three. I figured if we could have the level three locked down (under control) for years, with us being behind an electric fence, these guys on the minimum must have had it ten times better. Instead, they had it worse. They were completely dependent on other cars for drugs, tobacco, and cell phones.

This wouldn't do. I wasn't prepared to just sit back and have me or my car struggling when it was completely unnecessary. I started exploring options immediately.

I was able to work out a deal with a member of another car and agreed to help him get in some tobacco, and all but guaranteed its arrival, and that he would be five cans of Bugler richer at the end of it all. I continued my proposal by also throwing in a trustworthy connection on the level three. The guy on the level three was a Wood just like him. He could sell tobacco on the higher security yards for a heftier profit and take commission. That is, if he let me use his cell phone to organize it all.

After seeing in my eyes how confident I felt about it touching down on the yard, and having already heard of me, he agreed. I got started on my project.

The prison was over a hundred miles from where my family was living, making frequent visits difficult at best. During my incarceration, my parents had divorced. My little sister thought I was in school until she was about six or seven. When my mom would bring her on visits, she thought the white prison van was a school bus.

Families could come for a day, usually weekends, and we'd sit around and talk, play games with our families, use the vending machines in the visiting room, or order food from the prison café. The visiting area was a large, open room with seating and had a smaller outside area with ten-foot cinder-block walls.

I didn't know when I would get a visit most times. But when my family arrived—or my friend Crystal who is now my girlfriend—I'd get an announcement and some time to get ready. I would walk out to the front gate of our facility yard where the guard would pat me down and give me a ducket—a ticket, a slip of paper with my destination. I'd walk to the visiting area, go in one set of doors, strip out completely, and redress.

*Crystal, a longtime friend then and now
my girlfriend, visited me in prison.*

At the same time, my family was being searched. Women couldn't wear bras with underwires or bring in a purse, only a clear bag, and only a certain amount of money. No form-fitting clothing, nothing low cut. And it didn't happen to my family, but the guards could fuck with them and even request that the girls undress and squat over a mirror.

Once the visit was over, I was stripped out again. And back to my cell.

My mom and sisters visited me in prison.

The following paragraph contains allegations and I admit to nothing.

They allege that I breached the outer perimeter fence a couple weeks after my initial arrival to the minimum yard. The story goes that I was making my way back to the yard from having freshly returned from a certain drop spot. Allegedly shortly after my return, I began to make myself comfortable at my bunk and change out of my alleged escape gear. Allegedly while I was still breaking a sweat from the trek, certain fiends heard I had tobacco and refused to leave my bunk area even though it was now count time. This is where the officer allegedly began his contact with me.

I was actually chilling at my bunk, after a hard workout (not escape), politely asking someone to leave, and it was at that time when I was approached by the officer. My area was searched, and they turned up some tobacco and a new two liter of Hawaiian Punch. I denied ever seeing them there before and asserted that I had been set up, but, like, for real this time. They weren't buying it. They suspected me of jumping the fence, but could only prove possession of contraband.

Turns out they didn't sell two-liter sizes of fruit punch at the prison. The tobacco wasn't as big of an issue. They had only stopped selling it less than two years before. We were allowed to run through any existing amount we may have had, so it was a hard one for them to prove that it just wasn't an old stash. I was returned to the level-three yard for a few weeks and was then brought back to the minimum yard after a favorable disciplinary ruling.

I had solidified myself there. The dude who had trusted me with his phone saw firsthand I was no snitch. If he was skeptical before, he wasn't now. I took the fall and he didn't get hit. Even though it was expected of everyone to keep quiet, it was always good to be able to identify the solid ones. He saw that in me and was very accommodating whenever I asked to borrow his cell phone. He knew I was careful, had money, would return the favor with product, and wouldn't snitch if I got popped.

The homies were back on top in no time.

With the aid of another resourceful homie, we had shit sewn up and fully cracking (doing very well) within a month of my second arrival. I again looked out for the right people and would often send courtesy packages to the homies on the level-three yard, and also remembered to look out for the homies in the hole. This was the first time in years that someone had hit the minimum yard and remembered those that were left behind the fence. At least in a consistent manner anyway.

I knew all too well that my presence on the minimum yard could be short-lived. The other cars on that yard were used to having the upper hand. Not so much in numbers, but in hustle. So me being snitched on was a very likely possibility. Whether or not they caught me slipping was completely up to me though. Either way I knew if I were to land in the hole or the level-three yard again, I'd be looked out for.

I again made it a point to establish a solid circle of homies. The minimum was dormitory living, and a much harder environment to keep secrets. I was bringing in enough supplies to kick down certain people on my floor with care packages as well. I also had good homies to chill with during my time there. The homie Frosty from Sherman lived in my area, along with his homeboy Chino.

My homeboy Kartoon was on the yard now too. He lived in the other building, but would stop by our spot often and chill. The homie Scrappy from the River Bottom had even stopped by for a short visit at some point. Frosty from Escondido and Criminal from Linda Vista were always chilling too. The older homie Perico (Otay) lived in my building, but in a different area. He also liked to draw and paint, so I'd chill with him often and brush up on my art skills in the yard's hobby shop (only available on minimum facility, cheap bastards).

I would look out for political figures in other cars as well. They were surprised that I did this, considering we'd have to try and kill each other in a riot and all. It was done like this for the same reason I did it in the kitchen, to avoid being snitched on. Minimum yards had almost no political rules, and snitching was a massive problem there. I figured if I hooked up the top dogs, they may tighten up protocol to keep the love coming their way, and it worked. Often prisoners would just hang out in the cops' office with them, chopping it up. I hated seeing that. I felt like anyone who was that close to the cops couldn't be trusted and was probably snitching.

Things changed when a certain homie got to that yard. I won't go into too much detail, but he laid down the rules and shaped the yard into what it needed to be. A lot of homies that had been there prior to his arrival hated the new rules. They complained that he was making it too much like a higher-level facility. Regardless, things changed, and, surprise, the snitching became less widespread. I was now ready to get shit really taking off.

I don't know how, but two pounds of weed miraculously hit our yard. Smoking blunts became a daily thing. I would often gather the members of my circle and invite them to a smoke session. Blunts sprinkled with cocaine were a regular nighttime enjoyment. Finding any reggae CDs to borrow became a difficult task, but things seemed cool for the most part. I just couldn't help but think that it could all get better though.

I began having food and street alcohol delivered as well. On one beautiful night I received an order of fifteen Jumbo Jacks, two bottles of Jack, some tobacco, and a few Mad Dog twenty twenties (malt liquor). Life was definitely getting better. I had more cell phones ordered just to have on standby. I stashed them extremely well, and they were only to be removed if the others got discovered.

I remember having a carne asada cookout in my bunk area one lovely afternoon. I cut up pieces of the fresh steak and cooked it in three different metal hot pots I had going. I invited a few select people over for the feast and offered them nachos as they waited for the main course to be ready.

Of course we'd need something to wash all this goodness down with, so I busted out (removed) some Steel Reserve 211s from a three-gallon bucket of ice I had under the bunk and issued them out accordingly. We bumped a playlist of some gangster shit and smoked weed till we couldn't anymore. It was like the prison scene from *Goodfellas* where they were cooking lobster and cracking open bottles of red wine—except we were clearly on more of a budget. But, hey, I did what I could, you know?

I received word that the level-three yard had a massive crackdown, and all cell phones had been confiscated. Such crackdowns usually started with a surprise lockdown followed by ten to twenty guards coming into each building to assist with stripping out the prisoners from each cell one at a time. Then two officers would enter each cell to conduct the search while the inmates sat in the dayroom or yard area in their boxers. Mattresses were wanded with a metal detector, and all contraband was confiscated.

I had been through many of these crackdowns. An officer had once flung my thin mattress over the railing of the top tier to wand it with a metal detector. Each pass he made with the wand would trigger its alarm. He looked down at me as I sat in the dayroom just watching him. He waved the wand a few more times, and again he got a hit.

He looked very satisfied and confident of the fact that he had caught me with something. Except that he forgot the fucking railing was made of metal tubing. His next step would have to be cutting open my mattress to expose the treasures inside. I needed a new mattress anyway, so I just continued to watch.

He cut that mattress open like a rabid dog tearing into a stuffed animal and removed chunks of fluff one heap at a time. While the Mattress Ripper was going to town, I'd feed into his suspicion and insinuate I knew I was caught.

"Do they have HBO in the hole now?" I yelled up to him. "Do you guys get good reception in the hole? I'd like to know in advance if possible please."

When I finally informed him of where it was he went wrong with his investigation into my bedding, he didn't look too happy. I slept on a metal slab that night but had a new fluffier mattress the next day. I even got to use the extra fluff they left scattered in my cell to make a pillow. I counted it as a victory.

I made a few moves and had them another phone that week. The level three was back on track and the minimum yard was off the chain. I would love to go into further detail, but my time on the minimum yard all kind of blended together. I stayed high though. My favorite combination was heroin and weed. That combination made the days just fly by.

It wasn't long before the ISU was on me again. They would hit my sleeping area and building often. On one occasion they specifically mentioned the blunts I was apparently "known" to smoke. I denied all knowledge and passed all drug tests whenever they were administered (not telling how). This wasn't helping with the ISU's stress levels, I'm sure.

They actually hid themselves in an ambulance and drove it up to my building one night. The windows were big in minimum buildings, and I could see the vehicle approaching. I don't know why in the hell they thought I wouldn't notice a real ambulance (not the meat wagon) pulling up to the front of my building, but thank god for their tactical planner, right?

I noticed that no one was man down in the building so I stashed my items as the ambulance approached. Six to eight ISU officers came pouring out the back of the ambulance with nonlethal guns drawn. They stormed the building and commanded us all to get on our bunks and to stay there.

They came in so confident and assertive. I could tell they worked hard on this plan. Another bogus mission for them, I thought to myself. Poor guys. They again found nothing after a thorough search of the area and left the building noticeably frustrated. I could see the hate in their eyes as each one walked past me to exit the building, whispering to each other as they made the short walk back to their clown car.

We needed to celebrate our latest victory over the ISU so we began putting a list together of delicacies we'd like to have on our next delivery. Everything came through and we washed down our Famous Star burgers with bottles of the finest Cisco and puffed on blunts throughout the night. An item also included on the list was a disposable camera.

A homie had suggested we take a bunch of pictures and send the camera back out to the streets to have the film developed. Even though we had camera phones, we decided the disposable camera would offer clearer images. Also, you can't wiretap a disposable camera like you could a phone. So it seemed the wiser option, but I was high. It was all done in the hopes of gaining some new female connections and possibly getting a few to come up and visit at times.

We ate good food, got high, drank, and took as many pictures as we could. We walked through our dorm snapping photos of one another. I posed a couple times holding my bottle of Cisco up for the camera to see. Another homie allegedly took one while on the cell phone. We had an awesome night of good eating, drinking, and partying. We stashed everything and crashed for the night, but the camera would never make it back out to the streets.

The ISU came the next day and went straight to the stash spot, making my hangover suck even more. Apparently there was a hole in my area's bathroom ceiling that had previously gone undetected. The ISU sent a pocket-sized member of their squad up there to investigate. He spent about twenty minutes crawling and sifting around the tight area, handing one piece of contraband down at a time.

Poor-quality copies of the photos we took of that memorable night. Gooners kept the originals.

Someone had dimed us out, and it was my own fault for being careless. They seized the evidence they found. After developing the film in the camera, they were back the next day to pick up everyone who had been featured in any of the photographs.

Everyone but myself and the homie Chino from Sherman pictured on the alleged cell phone (I say it was a tiny Walkman) were cut loose to the level-three yard. Chino and I were taken to the hole. They wrote me up for being in possession of alcohol (which carried four months extra time) and suspicion of escaping. At my hearing I beat the alcohol charge citing lack of evidence, and they could never prove the escape. Yes I had a bottle of Cisco, but stated it was empty and only for show.

They got me on a contraband charge and retained me in solitary pending review. The homie Chino paroled a month and a half into our stay at the hole. The committee kept me back there for just over seven months, always with a hold pending review.

The hole sucked balls. I was stuck, and the care packages stopped. We received word that everything had stopped, because everything was found. There was nothing left to send, nor any resources available to get more. The cops hit the minimum and level-three yards and took it all.

And there I was, in the hole.

Hole is solitary, fucked-up purgatory. I got nothing. No TV. A metal bunk, a mattress, a blanket, a towel, a sheet, just the basics.

The hole is laid out like any other building. Only much more secure and completely isolated from the general population of the prison. I was cuffed or shackled or both at all times outside of the cell. If I was going to the yard, I was cuffed through the tray slot of my cell door before exiting. Then uncuffed once I was securely at my next destination—yard, shower, visitors, trips to the infirmary.

Sometimes I had a cellmate. Sometimes not.

For free time, I was taken to a cagelike yard of concrete and steel. I received no phone calls, not even if my mother was on her death bed. No contact visits, ever. All visits in the hole were behind glass. My family could only look at me through glass, while I was mostly shackled, and only one arm was unrestrained.

Our main source of physical contact for my stay there was the officers' latex gloves clutching my wrist as they placed the cuffs around them.

While in my cell, I just existed. That's the only thing I had going on. The random screams at night from distant cells reminded me of that. But I didn't exist to the outside world.

The criminal injustice system quotes inmate violence for better funding. If you only have razor wire, tattoos, cages, shackles, and screams to keep you company, you'd become a lot of things. Rehabilitated isn't on that list. Words like *hateful*, *angry*, *cold*, *antisocial*, and *numb* would fill the lines on that specific list.

My homeboy Puppet showed up a couple months into my solitary stay. He was short in stature, but vicious in nature. He stood maybe 5 feet 2, yet many people still feared him. He had beaten a double murder as a teenager and was believed to be responsible for another unsolved homicide. I knew him from the streets, and he had passed through Donovan on parole violations a couple times during my earlier years there. He gave no fucks about getting out. This time was no different, another violation, but if it ended up being life, so be it.

He told me he heard of the way I had shit popping off out on the yard and said he had received everything I sent his way on his previous stays. He was validated as an associate of a certain prison gang by then and therefore had to do all his time in solitary every time he came back. I asked him to relay a message for me and deliver a kite (note) to someone on the streets that owed me a favor. He was paroling any day and agreed to help me out. His day came and he paroled. I stayed stuck and continued to hold it down.

The cops that regularly worked the hole were jerks. The officers were responsible for serving our meals to us. A couple carts containing whatever pans of food were on the menu that day and empty food trays were delivered by the prison kitchen workers. The inmate workers would leave the food items in front of the hole for the officers to retrieve. The officers would then bring all items and carts inside and proceed to begin making our trays.

The fuckwads would only give us half portions though. If they ran out of food, they would have to order more from the kitchen and wait for it to arrive (so much work). This was far too much of a burden for the lazy fucks working in building seven (where I was housed) to handle. So to avoid running out, they would short the portions. I already had to put up with such things as lack of sunlight, people screaming throughout the night, and having no contact with the outside world. Now I'd have to deal with all that on an empty stomach.

Not only was the hole the most boring place on earth, but we were being starved. I began drawing again to get a few extra soups here and there, but it was rough. I needed to figure something out, but every resource I knew of was gone. Art would have to hold me down (be my main hustle) until I got out of the hole, whenever that was.

We were supposed to get one hour of yard per day and only be locked down twenty-three of those. The cops would keep us locked down twenty-four hours a day, three to four days at a time, and give us four hours of yard on the fourth day. One five-minute shower was allowed every third day. But if you pissed off these lowlife guards, they would kill the cameras and go to work.

I saw two poor bastards get put in cuffs through the slot on their cell door and brought out, after one officer had signaled the tower to kill the cameras. They cut the clothes off this guy's back with scissors and that of his cellmate as well. The guard and his crime partners then removed all items from the guy's cell, including toilet paper, blankets, and mattress, fucking everything. They put the guys back in the cell naked and with no supplies whatsoever.

The outside of their cell door was then blocked at the bottom with their own mattresses so no other inmates could attempt to deliver supplies by means of phishing (a long twine-like piece of line with a thin weight attached to one end that is slid into cells to deliver messages or supplies). I didn't know what those guys did, but the cops left them like that for three days. It gets cold in the cells. Normally it's manageable, but with no clothes or blankets, or anything for that matter, it must have sucked big-time at night. The circulation vents in the cells are all connected.

As people begin covering their vents (usually with paper and soap), the pressure of the incoming air becomes stronger and louder in the other cells and can make it difficult to hear your own cellmate only feet away. If you're the last cell during winter with no vent cover, you better have a solid plan of getting something on there. With no supplies or blankets for those guys to combat that kind of shit, they must have been suffering.

Last I heard, one of the cell's occupants had filed a complaint on the guard. Which is what brought his wrath down upon them. He made two people suffer for the minor inconvenience they had caused him with a write-up, and neither free staff (nurses, doctors mostly) or any correctional officers stopped it. So fuck all those staff members working in the hole at that time. You're part of the problem.

Puppet ended up coming back on a five-year term for drug possession. He moved into my cell, and we passed the time with old stories from the street. He got charged with stabbing a homie on the yard in the hole shortly thereafter and didn't seem to care that his five-year term might turn into ten or twenty.

Apparently a homie had masturbated in front of a nurse or female guard, and that was a no-go in there. Puppet allegedly took a razor blade to the now ex-homie and with surgical precision let him know how badly he'd fucked up for making the car look bad.

The yard in the hole at that time was a small maybe sixty-foot square of concrete. It had one toilet, three twenty-foot-tall cinder-block walls, and a fence with a gate for entry and exit to the yard acting as the fourth wall. A gunner in a tower was perched at one corner of the small, desolate concrete yard. The gate and walls were also lined with razor wire at the top for extra security.

I never really understood that seeing as how it was still very much prison on the other sides of those walls. Felt kind of like the state gave the California corrections people too much razor wire for Christmas one year and they just found a use for it.

There was no escaping the view of the gunner unless he was sleeping or distracted with his phone. Puppet was pretty much fucked. He frequently told me the story of when the masturbator screamed especially loud during the procedure. Puppet was on that particular yard when the alleged attack occurred, and the yard itself was incredibly small. Pretty hard for Puppet not to hear anything.

The cop allegedly saw everything and claimed to have also caught Puppet on the surveillance camera committing the alleged crime. I still don't believe it. Even with that being the case, Puppet seemed stress-free. He enjoyed planning future hustles. Even though I still had around two years to go (which is considered a short amount of time in there), and Puppet himself was looking at who the fuck knows how much more additional time on top of his initial sentence, he still liked to talk of the streets and potential hustles we could get into later on, when we were both out again.

I went in front of the committee for the sixth or seventh time, and yet again, I remained on hold pending review. The ISU sergeant would make it a point to be at damn near every committee I had. I could see him inside the room through the small window on the committee's metal door, preaching to them passionately and speaking with his hands as well.

Often he'd glare back at me through the small reinforced glass window during some of his performances. I would just sit backward in a chair, shackled at the waist with a guard hovering over me. I'd shake my head at him while maintaining eye contact. Obviously expressing my disappointment with him and his snitch tactics.

I call him a snitch because I considered him to be a criminal at that time too (probably still is, with his evidence planting ass). He knew he was a bitch, I'm sure. I knew for a fact he was. I would never have a chance by the time I made it in to talk to the committee.

"Do I feel like killing myself?" they would ask me. "Do you understand the committee's decision in retaining you in administrative segregation" is all I'd be asked. No outside agencies monitored conditions. Well none that are outside of the California correctional officers' control anyway. So that time, like all the ones before it, I remained in the hole, on hold, pending review.

As luck would have it, though, just five days later, a major riot broke out on the reception yard. I had gone through that reception yard, too, before landing on the level three years before. Reception yards are known to crack off (erupt into a riot) constantly. You have anywhere from your eighteen-year-old shoplifter with a prior type of person, all the way to your I've-killed-eight-people-and-bathed-in-their-blood people. So emotions are a little mixed, but everyone's definitely not in a zen-like state of mind. I'm sure on that.

The freshly convicted killers, or other lifers, are now overstressed, just got life, lost everything they've known and just have all of that shit stewing in their minds at all times. Now some kid doing six months for a marijuana conviction of another ethnicity or car affiliation bumps into the killer on the track after chow, but doesn't say excuse me. The kid thinks he's a tough guy, the killer thinks the kid reminds him of someone that testified against him. Ladies and gentlemen, you have yourselves a race riot.

The prison had hundreds of participants that needed housing in the hole. All people currently housed went up for emergency committee review, and I was kicked out back to the level-three yard because I wasn't there for violence. These fuckers, just days later when reviewing my file at emergency committee actually asked, "Why are you even back here?" while blundering through my file.

"I've asked that every time I've been here," I answered.

Puppet and I were both equally excited. He knew I could make things happen and quick at that. He stayed behind to hold things down that time. I hit the yard with one thing on my mind: to get shit flowing for myself and the homies again.

17
THA CROSSROADS

I HIT THE yard during the last unlock, right before chow (around 3:00 p.m.). People looked at me as though they'd seen a ghost. I probably looked like one too. I was down to about 150 pounds from being starved and pale from over six months of having no real sunlight.

Certain homies had heard I was validated; others thought I was fighting a new case. They were all surprised to hear that I had simply been fucked over by the ISU, but not too surprised. I vented about my ordeal for a while to the homies who had asked me about what happened, but then headed toward my block for a nice shower and, hopefully, a nice spread (prison food mixture based primarily around ramen noodles).

I entered my block and shit looked different. Two large rows of bunk beds had been installed in the dayroom on both sides of the building. I needed to hop on the phone and there was some dude's bed literally in my personal phone space. So now this guy gets to hear about my personal life, fucking great. He wasn't there at the time, so I phoned home to Mom and said hi for the first time in months. We planned a time for her to come down and visit with my sisters, had a conversation, and hung up.

The resident in the phone area turned out to be my younger homie Ghost. He was just passing through and would be paroling soon. He told me we had two other homies from the hood in the building as well named Shotgun and Lento. They were around his age too—the age I was when I first went in, only eighteen or nineteen. None of them had a considerable amount of time.

I was now over twenty-five years old and still had about nine months to go. I would be paroling after all of them. They informed me our homie Gumby was in another block as well. I'd have to see him at next unlock.

I asked them where the pruno was and who I needed to talk to about some drugs. I assumed they'd be pointing me in the direction of another car. Instead they pointed me in the direction of our own. I was shocked when I saw who it was. Because it meant the person slanging here was lying about being unable to send care packages our way in the hole. He knew me from previous years and was aware I had connections.

He spotted me, came down the blue metal stairs, and greeted me with heroin already in hand, my kind of service. I was still somewhat bothered by what I was seeing, but dropped the issue temporarily while I floated on a cloud.

Once that cloud slightly faded away, I began to get ready for chow. The hood was four heads deep now in the building, and we mobbed down to the chow hall together. We took up a table, and I began to tear through my tray like I had an eating disorder. I took every item down. One of those items was spinach. No one really ate that shit because it looked and tasted like I'd imagine lawnmower grass buildup does. Nevertheless I was taking all donations on spinach.

I explained to the homies how I was recently starved for over six months and that the torture had just ended. They said I definitely looked starved and hung with me until I finished eating my mounds of donated spinach.

We made our way back to the building, and I began to plot. I lay in a bunk that was once home to our wooden dayroom benches. Now there were potential enemies lying right next to me, all night. Plus we were easy targets for the gunner if shit were to crack off into a riot. All bad.

I talked with the right people and got into a cell pretty quickly. I moved in with the good homie Trusty from East Side. He was from a different hood but was a solid dude. He had hung out for a couple years early on in my sentence, and this was the first time I had seen him in almost three years. We got caught up, and I explained to him what living with me entailed now. He told me he had already heard of how the ISU fucked with me but understood the issue and seemed to be cool with it.

Everything on the yard got back on track soon. Packages were going where they needed to go, and the homies on the yard and in the hole were straight. Things weren't quite what they used to be, but I was staying on top of my hustle and also making the days fly by.

Trusty paroled eventually, and I moved the homie Lento into the cell. We were from the same neighborhood, and I figured he'd be the person I could trust most. I was right. Even though I had just met him, he kept any info from the cell between us, and we never got cracked.

The ISU had, oddly enough, not been sweating me. This was way unlike them. I was less than two months from paroling, so I figured they were just going to take my stay in the hole as their victory lap and let me go home. Seemed like a reasonable assumption on my part, but I was wrong.

I was set to parole on October 25, 2009. However on September 10, 2009, while eating cookies in my cell and watching *The Price Is Right*, my door began to open. The tower officer announced over the building's intercom that I had an attorney visit. This was highly suspect to me as I did not have an attorney at the time. I also knew the ISU office was located in the same area that attorney visits were held. I walked to the door and asked the officer to close it and told him I wasn't going.

He closed the cell door, and I watched him through my window. He was in a Plexiglas box with gun slots, so you could always see what they were up to. He hopped on the phone to inform the person on the other end that I had refused my "attorney" visit. The tower officer then hung up his phone and began to open my door for a second time.

I knew what was happening. The ISU was trying to trick me into going to their office, but this method of trickery was uncommon for them. They were more known for snatching you right off the yard in force.

My suspicion was they were trying to make it seem as though I went to their office voluntarily. I was also most likely not coming back if they were taking those steps to lure me there. If anyone voluntarily met with ISU, or any other officer for that matter, and were then taken to the hole during said meeting, it was assumed that person had requested to be placed in protective custody. So I concluded they were desperately trying to ruin my reputation for some reason. I knew they weren't fans of mine, but this move could have gotten me killed had their half-witted plan succeeded.

Once my door was fully open, the tower officer picked up the phone again and called down to the floor cop. The floor officer then shouted up at me and asked me to come down. I walked out of my cell and down to where he was now standing in the dayroom. He then proceeded to tell me in a whisper that the ISU had ordered that I go to their office. They must have been banking on me not wanting to get extra time for refusing a direct order. But someone must have forgotten to tell them I was *there* for bank robbery.

I told the floor officer I still wasn't going. He then fired back with, "They told me to place you into custody if you refuse," and began to remove his cuffs from his work belt. I said nothing and instead turned my back to him and held my arms out straight on both sides and waited to be placed in cuffs. He grabbed each wrist one at a time and cuffed me up.

A few minutes later a couple members of the ISU showed up to escort me to their bitch ass office. I was bent about the situation itself, but found some solace in knowing I had fucked up their original plan.

Arriving at the rats' nest (ISU office), I was sat down at a table opposite of an ISU lieutenant. He informed me that he was validating me as a prison gang associate and would be submitting his evidence to Sacramento in the form of a Validation Packet. I need some heroin, I remember thinking to myself. I really did though. I had been without for about three days, and I was scheduled to get hooked up later on that night. Wasn't gonna happen now.

The validation process is based off a point system. Three points you're validated, and off to the forgotten place. An example of a validation point could be a tattoo of prison gang affiliation, or if you are in direct contact with someone they consider to be a prison gang leader. The lieutenant advised me he only needed three points to put me away, but continued with, "I'm giving you four just in case you beat one of them." Such a bitch he was.

"How the fuck do I have four points?" I politely asked.

He began to list the points. Three were directly related to my homeboy Puppet and one was from a rat that claimed I was a member of the prison gang's ruling body known as La Mesa (The Table). So three points were because of my association with Puppet (who himself was only validated as an associate) and one was due to a singular rat saying I was part of something? Jesus Christ, our system isn't broken, my ass.

He then asked me to snitch on anything criminal I knew of, and in return I'd be released back to the yard as though nothing had happened. Those dudes had me fucked up.

I turned down his lame ass offer and asked to be taken wherever the next step was. Some of the ISU officers were doing their usual taunting bullshit when I was being placed in one of their holding cells to await administrative segregation (the hole) placement: "Bye Bandit" and "I didn't know you were a gang boss, Stanley?" to which I simply replied, "I'm not," and in turn was told "Well you are now!" which was then followed by an eruption of ISU laughter. I walked right into that one, fuck.

They once again deemed me a threat to the safety and security of the institution and held me pending committee review, or SHU placement. Funny how that same ISU officer could go around killing people, but I'm the one deemed a threat.

Arriving at the hole, again, I realized how upset they actually were with me. They placed me in a small white steel cage good for standing room only to strip out, but they put me in a cage on the side of the building that was considered "no good" (which signified I'd be housed on that side). I could be over there temporarily and move to the good side later, no problem.

The homies saw me arrive and would know to pull me over as soon as possible, but I'd be surrounded by enemies. I only had three days to submit a proper rebuttal and appeal my charges of prison gang association.

I would need to know about the appeals process in order to do so. Some inmates had mastered the appeals process, but I wasn't one of them, and Google sure as hell wasn't an option. I didn't know where to start, and it looked as though I'd have no help from anyone around me. Sure enough, right in the middle of the bad side I went—to perform a bunch of guesswork for what's technically an organized crime label on my jacket (arrest history/gang affiliation).

The bad side wasn't actually all that bad though. It came with such accommodations as half portioned meals, early morning chess matches from over ten cell lengths away where the moves would be shouted across the tier for any of the other chess fans' enjoyment, and random verbal attacks from some protective-custody inmates (snitches, rapists, and child molesters who were segregated from the general population because their safety was in jeopardy) disrespecting me and my car.

Inmates would graph out a chess board on a piece of paper and number the squares. They'd yell out their moves, usually at two in the morning, like an endless game of bingo while I was trying to sleep: "P twelve," "B ten."

Even though that side had so much to offer, there was still no one I could reach to help me with my appeal. Five days later I was transferred to the good side. I had winged the whole appeal and only hoped I did right.

If I did it wrong, I would be slammed no less than twenty-three hours a day and given yard (which at that point was and still is a two-man dog kennel) and never be allowed a contact visit again. No phone calls, no free movement outside the cell, cages, shower, or kennel. Just always shackled and under escort while in between them.

Also any crimes I commit thereafter can be looked at as though I'm carrying it out for the prison gang, which means potentially up to a life sentence as enhancement on top of my original charge—all for being an associate of a prison gang. Yet they had only proven me to be an associate of an associate and referred to the same person for three points. Where the fuck does that train stop?

On the way to the hole, an ISU officer asked me a question: "You hear about your homeboy Puppet?"

"What about him?"

He told me that Puppet had overdosed in his cell and had died as a result. I was left to ponder that for all of thirty seconds as we pulled up in a golf cart (most common mode of transportation for staff) to the front of the same building I had left not too long ago, and the same building Puppet had just died in.

The buildings are all the same on the outside in the higher levels. Concrete with no paint, and a couple fogged windows for natural light high up. At the front of the building there's dirt and patches of grass. Then a blue steel door slides open and shuts remotely from within the building's tower. Behind that door is the sally port (hallway underneath the building's gunner tower), then a steel cage door that also remotely slides open to expose the building's floor plan.

Dismal enough, now I'd have to mourn my homeboy while staring at his exact place of death until I paroled. If that was even still going to happen.

18
MASTERS OF WAR

PUPPET NEVER SPOKE too much about his personal life, but I know he loved his family. During my last ad-seg stay, he would sometimes flip through his personal photos and show me some of his favorite memories with family.

Just above his shaved hairline on his forehead was a tattoo in bold print that read "LEFT BEHIND" (signifying he'd accepted he would be left behind during the rapture if it were to occur). The words were wedged between two tattooed devil horns that would always stand out as he proudly handed me a picture explaining to me who it was, and what the picture's backstory was. I could tell he was longing for his family, but he never let it show beyond staring at a photo for longer than usual.

About his death, I found out someone had kicked him down some new shit, he took a little too much, and his cellmate didn't know how to respond to his overdose. I'm not exactly sure what happened, but it seemed like no one knew how to tackle the problem. Do you inform the building officer your cellmate has overdosed on heroin and risk him surviving, and you then become the reason he gets more time for drug use? Will your cellmate be appreciative, or accuse you of snitching on him?

No one wanted to risk being labeled a snitch. By the time someone stepped up and had them call man down, it was too late. Puppet was gone. From the sounds of it, an ISU officer tried his best to perform CPR, but again, too far gone by then.

We lost homies from the hood often enough, it was nothing new. A homie who had been with me on the minimum yard recently lost his sixteen-year-old little cousin Shrek from Otay on the outside. A couple people walked up to him and some of his family members at the park. One person asked if anyone present was from Otay. Shrek quickly stated to the mystery people that he in fact was.

They shot him down right there in front of his family members, and he died in their arms. I heard that at least one of the two people snitched on the whole deal. Apparently they were new recruits from a rival hood, allegedly following orders from a clearly wiser member to go out and get a member of Otay.

I never had the pleasure of meeting Shrek, but from what the homie had told me of him, I wish I had. He could've accomplished so much. If the type of effort and money they put into keeping Beverly Hills the way it runs and looks were put into Otay, and places like it, for just one year by our awesome representatives, some lives *would* be saved.

Gumby lost his cousin Gizmo from Otay Rasta Locos. All I heard was Gizmo was in a hotel with someone when they got a knock at their door. Gizmo walked to the window near the door and began to pull back the curtains to look outside. He was immediately shot. He was a solid ass homie and loved by many. Whoever pulled the trigger was lucky that Gizmo didn't see them coming. That's probably exactly what they were afraid of though. A fair fight. He was only twenty-two.

We don't live sheltered lives in the hood, and the fear of being shot when going to the store is a daily concern. Our American terror levels are always set to high alert. That's how we live in our day-to-day, and it sucks. But to hear of a homie dying in prison is extra depressing, and now they were trying to use his name to lock me up in the SHU for good.

Not only were three of my validation points based on Puppet, but he had passed two weeks before I had been placed in solitary for my association with him. Something like this is allowed to happen because of the CCPOA (California Correctional Peace

Officers Association) and strength of their union. It's very hard to get rid of a crooked guard in California, believe that shit. Their case against me was bullshit, but I wasn't familiar with the appeals process and how to properly search out relevant rules and regulations to mount a proper defense. So I just hoped I did it right and would parole on schedule.

For me, it was back to burpees, Navy SEALS, and a list of other exhausting workouts on an almost daily basis, just a few cells down from where Puppet had passed. I personally thought these self-imposed workouts in the cages sucked. Only because the floors of those things aren't exactly polished concrete. It was like sandpaper in some cages. As luck would have it, I experienced these cages often.

We homies performed these mandatory workouts as a group. Without a yard, we'd shout in our individual kennels as loudly as possible during workouts. Someone would lead. We'd start with 113 burpees and 113 jumping jacks. Then arm rotations and helicopters. We'd do military-style Navy SEALS—form of burpee that alternates right and left legs (look it up), usually 513 of these.

No tennis shoes were allowed back there. We were issued "Jap Flaps" while staying as a guest in the hole, and they love to slip off constantly during workouts. Just picture a ninja's foot. They look like that, but no gap in the toes and Jap Flaps have about a quarter-inch sole. I don't mean to come off culturally insensitive either. I literally never heard them referred to as anything else but Jap Flaps by inmates or guards.

Also notice how I say *guard* and not *peace officer*? These fuckers like to play "I'm a peace officer!" on every issue from trivial matters to the more serious staff assaults.

"Whose word are they gonna believe, yours or a peace officer's?" I heard that shit too damn often, but it was true. They've literally built a sadist fantasyland. Correctional peace officers are fired just like anybody else, when they get caught too red-handed, that is. The last story I had heard, and read about of a correctional officer being fired for anything other than smuggling contraband, was for sexual misconduct. At my very prison.

Don't go having any fantasies about some hot guard with double Ds sucking dick for compliments either. It was in fact some dirt bag/human being so-called peace officer male guard forcing some inmate to suck his dick. The inmate saved some of the guard's cum in a tissue and snuck it to his sister during a visit. They had it submitted as evidence, and testing began.

Apparently the officer had threatened the inmate into a regular blow job by saying he'd spread rumors on the yard of him being a snitch. Pretty fucking sick, right? Took a while for his unemployment status to become official, but that's about what it takes to get rid of a bad one. Nothing short of concrete evidence, because of their union.

Some guards even survive concrete evidence and just pop up at a different prison, guarding other people. Like the officers who instigate the gladiator fights. A lot of them kept their jobs I heard.

Yet a jury can be told to make a decision on an inmate's life based simply on a guard's word over the inmate's own, and often at that. Knowing damn well if there was an actual emergency in a public setting, no one, literally no one, would ask for a correctional officer to lead the charge on the investigation/search recovery efforts. Fucking nobody. Get over yourselves. You're high-paid security guards, not fucking first responders.

Most guards are like sadistic little hamsters in a plastic bubble of union and legal protection—with your fucking snipers in place before every conflict, gas throwing, armor wearing, shield carrying, swinging for heads with your batons, waiting for major backup before doing anything, soft ass selves. I know some people that'll do that job for minimum wage, plus benefits maybe, with all those cushions in place. They're not tough despite what some would have you believe. A more accurate word to describe them would be *pretentious*.

It's all a scam. Look into how these fools can play the system and walk away with over six figures a year (start with overtime), and still bitch about being underpaid. Look into how many guards are killed each year by inmates (in California) and compare it to how many inmates are killed each year by guards. Just Google that. If we so much as get in a fight with each other in there, we stand the risk of being shot down by a sniper. You'd be surprised at how a high-powered rifle in six different locations on the yard, surrounding you at all times, can level the playing field.

Yet they claim the need for more money from taxpayers to combat the inmates' growing numbers. A large portion of inmates in California are nonviolent, yet are spending years in prison as a form of punishment for trivial charges. Why not start there and eliminate the growing numbers problem altogether? I mean fuck rehabilitation, right? Ain't no money in all that nonsense I guess. Or else why has it not been done yet?

Why the fuck do our teenage youth need to go through the prison system for shoplifting or drug possession? Can't we just try and deal with that shit a few other ways before throwing their teenage asses in prison? Oh yes, you better believe that they will throw very young people away too, kids in fact. When they still sold tobacco, the prison canteen list specifically stated that any inmates under the age of eighteen were not permitted to buy tobacco products.

My homeboy Viper had been one of those child inmates. At sixteen he was charged as an adult and presented with a deal for a longer stretch (amount of time) in the Youth Authority, or a shorter one with the OGs in state prison (OGs are the original gangsters, the homies who came before you, veterans). He said fuck it and signed for prison. I don't recall what the charge itself was, but the sentence was short enough for him that time around. He wasn't fighting a murder, I know that. So why throw Viper away so young? What form of rehabilitation was he presented with?

No one walks away from their purses anymore, and no bank just sets a pallet of money out for the nonarmored truck to get later on that night. We're all very much aware that there are crackheads and thieves everywhere. Forgive me if I don't believe in your system of correction and rehabilitation and all, but I still don't get how that solves shit. You're taking our thieving, drug addicted, most poor citizens and fine-tuning their downward trajectory. Then you throw them away, fucking literally. *You* failed *us*, broken system, not the other way around.

I applaud the CCPOA for their hustle though. Make guards peace officers and it creates a need for higher spending to account for the union wages and benefits. To keep it all profitable, they just had to plan out a system where one entity (the state) would lock up the impoverished (the ones that have it worse than anyone else in the US) and make money off of them instead of "paying them" to stay on the street in the form of state-government-funded programs. A win-win for the state and CCPOA.

Now the state saves money and simply diverts profits (and the poor) over to keep the CCPOA happy. Check out the first sentence I came across while reviewing their lame website: "The mission of CCPOA is to fight on behalf of *our members* for the enhancement of wages and benefits, as well as the provision of a positive work environment."

Now I'm all for union wages and benefits, but nothing about protecting or serving on their minds there, just a hustle.

Now here's the very short mission statement of the California Peace Officers Association (real peace officers): To serve California law enforcement leaders by providing a focused resource for leadership development and personal growth and to advocate on behalf of all peace officers in order to support the mission of law enforcement and ensure the safety of our communities.

See the difference?

So why are the prison guards called peace officers? It's an undeserving title for members of an undeserving disruptive group with money on their minds. They're one of the most influential unions in California but remain low-key and out of sight. They donate millions to help sway elections in their favor. They're directly profiting off people going to and staying in prison. Even down to the only items and services an inmate can purchase in order to speak with their family members, and the food they can eat. CCPOA gets a cut of it all.

As Bob Dylan said in his song "Masters of War," and I paraphrase here, when you die, it won't matter how much money you made, you can't buy back your soul. And they called me a criminal.

So anyway I had feet that were being sandpapered is what I was getting at, and it was unpleasant. And that's my rant about the system. Thank you for listening.

Now it's time for me to get out. October 25, 2009, arrived and I was starved, pale, in need of a shave, and ready to parole. Not ready in a sense like rehabilitated, but my turn was up. Oh, I tried getting into an optometry program on my yard in 2003 or 2004 and succeeded in doing so, only to have it, and all the other trade programs, closed months later due to state budget cuts. So I did try.

Lucky for us we had certain homies who would take it upon themselves to teach willing participants math, English, and history. Like Memo from Maravilla (a big Viking-looking Mexican) or Raymond Solis (three-strike lifer/old cellmate), or Richard Ramirez (not that one/good guy/lifer). There's not enough programs geared toward the rehabilitation of inmates to justify the *R* in CDCR (California Department of Corrections and *Rehabilitation*). Just saying.

I had the concept about me that crime was bad, and I shouldn't commit it, but no real words of advice or guidance from my captors on how to integrate back into society. None. No programs. No guidance. Nothing. So like all adventurous things, I winged it. I was stripped down one last time during the parole process, for old time's sake I guess, given state-issued parolee garb, and driven out of the prison in a white van.

A few other parolees and I were driven in a hurry, in fact, down Highway 905 and dropped off at the Iris Avenue trolley station located in South San Diego. I believe there was a football game on and the guard wanted to get back to it ASAP. The corrections officer handed me a white envelope that contained $200, a mugshot of myself, and a bus token. He then instructed me and the others to get on the next trolley going our way so he could get back.

I did as instructed and hopped on the next one headed north. I was only going up a couple exits and getting off at the Palomar stop, which would put me within walking distance to the hood.

A transit officer boarded at the stop before mine, and I realized I hadn't purchased a trolley ticket. Shit! I had heard stories of people getting busted only hours after their release but never understood how that could really happen. I was technically only out for less than fifteen minutes by that time, so I could have very well set a new record. But the ticket machine looked like something from the future. I'd been inside that long. Things changed. I didn't know how to turn that bus token into a trolley ticket.

My mom was originally going to pick me up from the prison, but her seven-year heads-up alarm appeared to have been lost to a rogue phone update. I'd have to tell her ten years in advance next time, I thought to myself, when seeing she wasn't waiting outside the prison. She won't like that joke.

I was wearing tan prison parole pants, with an elastic waistband, a white T-shirt, and Jap Flaps. So combined with my paleness, thinness, and need for a shave, I looked like an insane person who had just crawled out of a hole (which I had) as I sat next to some people on the trolley. It was true in a way, though. Compared to the people around me, I probably was insane.

But I was just trying to get home, not eat someone's face. Blending in wasn't going to work, but the transit officer never even glanced my direction. He was already all over someone at the opposite end of the car.

We pulled up to the Palomar exit and I jumped off in a hurry. I walked over to a nearby Target and called my mom from a payphone in front of it—the same Target that was once a source of income for my juvenile self actually. She arrived with my sisters in tow less than ten minutes later. We all said our emotional hellos and gave our hugs, then stopped at Los Taquitos, my favorite taco spot. It had been over three months since I had something from there. Prison staff could be bribed to bring my carne asada burritos in with their food to keep me happy, so I would keep paying them for the bigger stuff.

After I ate, we stopped by to see my good friend Boomer to say hello. I hadn't seen him since sentencing. His was living with his wife out in the foothills of Bonita. After a few hours of catching up, we said our goodbyes.

We began the drive up to Lakewood where my mother was then living with my sisters in a two-bedroom apartment. I just sat back and soaked in the view of the Pacific as we continued on through Oceanside. It was cool to be out. But everyone knows it doesn't last forever. Damn near everyone goes back. It was common knowledge in the pen. I just knew I was going to do everything in my power to make freedom last as long as possible.

My sisters were then nine and fifteen and shared the second bedroom, so I had the couch. After about the two-thousandth time my younger sister, Veronica, played "Paparazzi" by Lady Gaga on the living room television while bouncing around on the sofa next to me, I knew I needed a job.

Finding a job and being able to get my own spot were going to be critical to my sanity. Not only would I get a break from Lady Gaga, but I wouldn't have to worry about ISU kicking in my door. Oh yeah, if you're a documented prison gang associate, the ISU can enter your residence with your parole officer. So I still had to worry about them bothering me out here too.

19
WANNA BE A BALLER

I HAD ALWAYS told myself I'd never flip burgers for money.

But I applied to every burger spot I could find and was denied each time. Denied across the whole board. I got turned down by smiling clowns and yellow stars and archways alike. The fall of 2009 was still very much recession ravaged. Work was damn near impossible to get, anywhere. My brand new twenty-something felony convictions weren't helping either. Plus I was twenty-six with no current work experience.

I told myself I wouldn't rob banks anymore, for my family's sake. It had hurt them in a major way to see me go. I could always remember seeing my mother's soul break when that judge gave me the maximum allowed during sentencing. I didn't want to repeat that process.

Lucky for me, a family friend named Paul M. was a member of the Los Angeles Ironworkers Union (Local 433). He was a superintendent with his company and had juice. He got me in the door, hooked me up with all the tools I'd immediately need for my type of job assignments, and I hit the ground running.

I showed up on time every day, and early at that. Well, after the first very loud and public ass chewing for being two minutes late, I was on it. The only circumstances of tardiness or absence were completely out of my hands if they were to occur. I needed that job. I couldn't afford to get fired during the recession and risk having to seek work based on months of experience. Fuck that.

I was a structural ironworker apprentice and had to get used to heights real fucking quick. My biggest fear of them to date was of being thrown off the top tier in a riot. This was a lot sketchier than the top tier. I hated heights, but adapted as quickly as I could. I definitely wasn't the type of dude that would be running across eight-inch-wide steel beams.

The back injury I sustained from my younger days while running from that sheriff had been catching up with me slowly over the years, and about a year into ironworking, it was fucking killing me. There were days I couldn't stand up on my own after lunch. I had to keep it quiet and discreetly ask for someone to help me out.

I couldn't wait for unemployment or disability either. I had saved enough to move into my own apartment by then and had bought a new Dodge Ram. I had bills to pay and goals to achieve. Going anything over three weeks without pay wasn't going to cut it. I just pushed through and tried to save as much as I could in the process, hoping to have enough cash put together someday soon to start my own business. I wasn't exactly sure what kind of thing I'd be starting, but figured I'd know it when I saw it.

By condition of parole I couldn't travel more than fifty miles from my legal address. This rule, I suspect, is designed to screw people into paroling to the exact same setting they were in before incarceration and then punishing them when they try to get out. It's most common for new parolees to list their parents' home as their address. The parents' homes were usually paid off and in the same hood they grew up in, so they were trapped in the same everything they were, just like before.

Above the fucking entrance to our jails and prisons, it may as well read, "Abandon all hope ye who enter here."

My paroling to Lakewood, however, saved me from that trap. At over a hundred miles from Otay, I knew no one in Lakewood, and there were no signs of gang activity. I had kicked heroin during the first week of my last solitary stay and never looked back. All the friendships I had developed since being out were from Local 433 (my union).

In the hood and among the homies it was almost expected for us to be the best, most-efficient *criminal* possible, the best gang member possible. If that's not what you were doing, then you could be considered dead weight and shit gets rough for you.

In the ironworkers union it was all about being the best, most-efficient *worker*. Unemployed union members would line the perimeter fences of our worksites in the mornings and at lunch by the dozens at times. They would arrive ready to work, with tools in hand. All they needed was for someone to get injured, or fired, and a spot would be available.

Seeing these guys damn near every day just waiting for a chance at my job kept me on my toes. The work itself was tough, very tough. Structural ironworking is one of the deadliest jobs in the United States. It's also got to be one of the most strenuous. The work is done in a fast, efficient, and safe manner, but everything is made of fucking steel. On 105-degree days when the sun is beating down on the iron, this can suck balls, immensely.

Every piece of steel sitting in the sunlight would be hot to the touch, which made carrying it, or sitting on it, that much suckier. Management instructed us to always have assistance picking up items over seventy pounds, but the first time I saw a coworker throw a beam that weighed more than a hundred pounds over his shoulder and continue on his journey, I threw that rule out the window. The way I saw it was that if I couldn't pick up heavy-ass shit on my own, then one of the people waiting outside the perimeter probably would.

Having a bad back wasn't helping me be the best ironworker I could be. In fact the pain was becoming unbearable. It's hard to carry thirty-six boxes of four rolls per box welding wire, one after the other, up four flights of stairs while your back is constantly asking you, "How the fuck are you walking right now, don't you feel these various pain signals?"

In July 2012, just under three years out of prison, I was unable to ignore those signals anymore.

One dark, early morning while sitting on my bed, and putting on my work boots, I sneezed. I felt something very wrong, a pain that was somewhat familiar, but more intense. It was a challenge to stand up, but I managed it. I slowly walked to my truck and began the drive to Glendale where my job site was located. It was a rough drive but I made it. The pain had been intensifying throughout my hour-and-a-half journey.

Part of my duties as an apprentice was to fill up the welding machines with cans of gas. Each can contained five gallons, and I would typically carry one in each hand as there were multiple machines throughout the job site that needed filling. I could already barely walk but figured if I pushed through the pain, I may loosen my back up. Nope. I picked up those cans and that was it. I crouched down to grab both handles, clutched them in my hands, stood up, walked a few steps, and could go no further.

I told my foreman Steve C. that I was in bad pain and needed to go home to rest up so I could hit it hard tomorrow. He could see I wasn't bullshitting and excused me. Work began for my coworkers, and I began the three-block walk of misery back to where I was parked. I began limping, but made it off the job site decent enough.

Now I had to get to my truck. It took me almost an hour to get through those three blocks. I couldn't call a coworker because they might report my true condition to our supervisors, and, again, I needed that fucking job. After several breaks I made it back to the truck and then home. I lay in bed with excruciating pain that only seemed to get worse. I just needed some sleep and I'd be fine, I thought to myself.

Throughout the night and into the morning I realized how wrong I actually was. I couldn't fucking walk. Not without a lot of assistance anyway. If I so much as twitched my right foot, I'd get a burst of fresh, horrible pain from my lower back down to my ankle, which would then take another thirty minutes on average for the pain to mildly subside. Simply resting it and pushing through appeared to no longer be an option, just as walking seemed to no longer be an option. I could do nothing but lie there and think. I had some help.

My sister Alexis had moved in with me when my mom got a job transfer to Alabama. She would help with cooking and anything else needed. A mutual friend would help when she was unavailable. Things like using the bathroom and bathing were extremely difficult. It was hard to figure out what my next move would be when I myself couldn't do much moving.

I notified work about what was happening and asked for some time to get back on my feet, literally. After a couple weeks I could get around on crutches, but my back had become deformed looking. The arch in my lower back was no longer curved. I was also leaning forward and my spine had curved to the side. The pain was intense, and my ironworking career seemed to be in serious jeopardy.

The guys at work put a collection together for me, and a fellow apprentice dropped by to leave me around $500. It was greatly appreciated, but I needed to think of next month and the ones that followed.

Seeing the doctors at first wasn't much help. They prescribed me lots of Norco, Vicodin, and muscle relaxers. Normally these prescriptions would be much appreciated, but I needed a fix to my problem, not just a high. The pills helped with the pain, but not the symptoms.

Another problem was that pain killers contain opioids, and so does heroin. I'd been off heroin for three years, but I still seemed to have a tolerance and enjoyment for opioids. But hey, doctor's orders. I asked for surgery every time I visited the doctor's office but would only receive a new prescription. Again, the pills did help keep the pain manageable, but I needed to work.

Being a drugged-out disabled person was not looking or feeling good, especially when a fix (surgery) was just an insurance approval away. No money in that, though, only a loss for the insurance company. They had me feeling like the cracked-out junkie from an early 1990s war on drugs television ad campaign. I had no other options.

So with my new pills, I retreated to an old familiar cloud I used to float on in prison and fucked around on Facebook. I didn't have a television in the bedroom and had no home cable or internet. So I just spent hours on my cell phone (and its unlimited data plan) surfing around the social media platform looking for old friends from school to see what had become of them.

Most of my closest homies were still busted. Frosty from Otay had just got broke off, along with the good homie Smurf. Some homies were arrested in an indictment less than two years before I got out. The lightest term given to one of my boys was eight years.

The homie Boomer, on the other hand, had started his own Hispanic cultural clothing line, Mesheeka Clothing. I had been investing with him prior to my injury, but the project was still in its beginning stages. So he was busy and the young company had yet to pull a profit. Ironworkers are real big on the work hard/play hard mentality. Since I couldn't really do the party thing at the time, or drive, I'd just stay home and medicate.

While at a get-together with some ironworkers a few months prior to my back going out, I had met a dude named Chris. I got to talking with him while outside smoking a cigarette and asked what he did for a living. He told me he had an office in Garden Grove and owned his own marketing business. He already knew I was an ironworker by just looking at me. I was still dressed in my work clothes as I had headed straight over to the party from the job site. He seemed pretty cool and we exchanged Facebook information, and I'm very glad I did that.

Three weeks into my ordeal, I regained the ability to drive. It was still extremely painful due to my back being very much twisted up. Driving longer than twenty minutes was almost impossible; my back wouldn't allow it. The pills kept me up at odd hours. I was again bored out of my mind, in pain, and using opioids. I hated being bored. Facebook only offered so much, and my sister had started working so most of the time it was just me.

I would often see that guy Chris online and decided to hit him up and see what he was doing one night. It was about two in the morning when I shot him a message. His response back was quick, and he had remembered me from the get-together and was glad to hear from me. During our conversation my criminal past had come up, and he was surprised to hear what I had done. It either interests people or scares them away. I try my best to avoid having it come up in conversation, but Chris had asked what I did prior to ironworking and kind of fished it out of me.

I figured no big deal if he knew, as all my coworkers already did. I asked what he was up to, and he informed me that he was at work. I asked him what in the actual fuck he was marketing at two in the morning and slid in, "Can I cruise by?" To which he responded with LOL, followed by an address, and "come through."

I grabbed my crutches and hobbled my way to the Dodge. This staying-at-home shit was becoming too much for me. Plus bills were due and I was down to my last $1,300. My truck and rent were $1,600 combined, and I was tired of thinking about it.

Chris seemed cool, and I figured since he was a businessman I might be able to pick up free game through conversation. I pulled up to his office and knocked on the suite number he had given me. A young woman opened the door and invited me in. I could see Chris in an interior office only a few feet to my right. His office door was open, and he appeared to be texting someone, vigorously. The young woman closed the door behind me and walked into a back office.

I saw myself to Chris's desk and sat in a waiting chair opposite him. He was still texting, angrily now. He wasn't letting his discontent for the person on the other end of his messages escape me either. He looked up and said, "This motherfucker thinks I'm stupid!"

I paused, processing. "Why do they think you're stupid, Chris?"

As he began to explain, a text came in. He looked at it, shook his head in an approving manner, and wrote the number 700 down in a column on a sheet of paper below some other figures. His mood changed and he asked me how I'd been and what the fuck happened to me. I filled him in on the issue with my back and told him I was in the process of getting it fixed. We began talking about his Mustang when another text came in.

Shortly after reading it, he wrote down the number 500 in a column of what I now realized was just one of seven. They had a pair of names written at the top of each column.

"What is that?" I asked. "What are those numbers?"

"That's how much money the company just made."

"So that text you got five minutes ago was a seven-hundred-dollar kind of text?"

"Oh yeah," he replied and nodded his head in his own approval.

"What the fuck do you do?" I asked, as I wore a face of shock and confusion.

"I do marketing for exotic dancers and escorts,"

This was it! This could turn it all around for me. Fuck yes, world of marketing, and I accept what you have bestowed upon me, Jesus baaaaaaaaby.

I was extremely fascinated to say the least. Chris didn't appear to be doing much work. Just constantly on his phone and computer. Just the kind of gig I needed at the time. I began to ask him a series of what may have been dozens of questions. He answered them all, no hesitation. How much would it cost to open up my own? He told me the list of items one might need to start something official like his and gave me a rough estimate of $12,000. Fuck. Out of my budget.

As he began focusing on the computer screen, clicking away with the mouse, he stated, "A lot of people have told me they want to do this, and never follow through."

After some thinking I replied, "Would you help me out with getting started if I was to open one up, like with advice and information?"

"Sure! But it isn't all that easy," he warned.

I continued to gather information by the mounds from Chris over the next two days. I'd cruise by during his shift and chop it up (converse). I kept the questions coming his way and ran through several scenarios, asking what the outcome "should" be in each one. He almost took my questioning as a challenge of his own knowledge regarding his field. He thought everything through and gave me good, reasonable answers.

I knew I could do that shit. It sounded like a sick-ass hustle, and it was all legal. I asked two friends from local 433 if they'd lend me money for my car payment. They both agreed and both even drove it down to me. I now had a grand total of $1,750 to my name.

I had sized up Chris's operation and figured if I'd simply cut a few costs and not be so selective on the area of the office location, I might be able to swing it. Something halfway decent at around $650 a month, max $1,300 down. I'd have $450 remaining but that would hardly be enough to activate services and furnish the office.

I took two days to figure out a plan on my budget. Whatever the plan was, it would still result in one definite conclusion, I was going all in. Sit back and pay bills until there's nothing left? I couldn't do criminal stuff even if I wanted to, I wouldn't be able to run if needed. This was making sense to me, so dollars must be following.

One thing I did have, after almost three years of being out, was good credit. I had no debt when I got busted. I had a clean slate and built from there on union wages and kept up on all bills. Local 433 changed my life. With that good credit score I was approved for a $2,000 credit line at a local electronics store. I had everything I needed. So no more thinking, I moved on it.

I called around on classified sites and checked prices for offices. The most affordable locations were in Los Angeles County. Affordable definitely didn't mean safe where I landed either. The outside wasn't so aesthetically pleasing at the location I settled on, but the building itself was well kept. I found a spot right around my price range near a freeway exit and signed a lease that day.

All they needed was a credit check and my last year's tax returns. No problem. I still had a damn near 700 score since my new credit line wouldn't yet be registered in the system, and my tax refund from work would cover the amount needed for the term of the six-month lease. I was approved then and there. I began the drive home and gave Chris a call.

I informed him of what I had planned, and of what I actively had in motion. I told him I was about to go to the store and spend my card on computer equipment and furnishings and asked if he'd still help me as promised. He was surprised. He asked if he could call me back and I told him it wasn't a problem. Around ten minutes later he called back.

"Are you serious? You got an office?" he asked.

"Oh yeah, I'm on it." The work wouldn't be a problem, and I had all other key ingredients to success lined up. Finding contractors to work with (exotic dancers or companions) was the tricky part. Chris had also warned me of that during our previous conversations. I could handle it, I figured, especially if Chris helped on further details of operations—a more general direction of where I should be pointed.

Once he was sure I wasn't fucking around, he ran me down on an idea he'd been having. He'd wanted to expand but didn't want to risk the full investment on his own at the time. Since I seemed serious about my money and trustworthy, he offered to partner with me on the new company. However, I'd be responsible for hiring, scheduling, and dispatching out the calls during work hours. I knew how much I could make off my resources alone, and I had it figured out to around $200 a day profit within two weeks, maybe less time if I had several girls calling daily.

But with Chris as a business partner, I'd be 50/50 of a winning system immediately. Profits could be around $300 a day within the first week if I kept on hiring contractors. Spending over seven years in the California prison system had taught me something critical—business skills. There's so much hustle and swindling going on in prison that spending enough time there will teach you how to better recognize when someone is trying to manipulate you in a deal. We call it running game.

If someone is trying to run game on you in prison, they're attempting to manipulate you. I much preferred when someone was putting me up on game (giving me knowledge). Seven years of hustling in prison had me dealing with some very manipulative personalities, especially when I had my own hustles going.

Everybody always wanted something, and some would promise the world to hopefully sway your decision.

I would be amused when certain people would give me their word that they'd pay me on their next canteen day (prison commissary). Yes we had regular once-a-month canteen draws, but if a riot cracked off, or the indebted inmate were to get in a fight, no canteen for me. Or when people just simply tried to sell me on their *palabra* (word). I was aware of unavoidable circumstances being able to happen at any moment, and that just is what it is. However I was also aware that one's word can't be kept in those situations, because they'd be in the hole, so how can they give me their word? They couldn't.

Sometimes inmates would try to fish information out of me in regard to my personal inventory, to better know what to ask for. But if they got any information, they would then tell the person they trust most. Then those homies would do the same, and BOOM, what do you know? I got a prison guard saying he's received my phone bill in the mail.

So I was aware everyone wasn't a potential snitch, but I knew people liked to brag to others about their accomplishments, and that bragging could take me down. Using a cell phone in prison is one of those kinds of things. Again, I had a tight circle for a reason.

Small things like that helped me recognize who was being sincere and who was running game. If they put no thought into how they approached me or the words they chose to use, they got nothing from me. Usually everyone got something kicked down for free at some point anyway. I looked out often for those who appeared to be struggling so they could make some money, or just relax. Everyone deserves to be treated with some level of compassion. If I had it a certain way and could spare some kickdowns for free, then I'd proceed to kick people down.

These qualities served me well because adult marketing was all hustle and game. The bookers would hustle clients while making the client feel they're winning the negotiation. Contractors would attempt to hustle us by attempting to pocket the company's money at times, saying nothing was collected from the client. A few logical points later and they'd find the money. Just got to know what to look for. Reverse engineer the scam.

I took Chris up on his offer. He trained me on how to dispatch calls to contractors, where to advertise, how to hire contractors, and how to communicate with the people out in the field. My back was injured in the middle of July 2012. By the end of August of that same year I owned my own adult marketing agency. I put my last $300 into advertising costs for the first night of work.

It took me a few days to get my first girl hired, but even though the company only had one girl, the company still had to run. We had girls that answered the phone from home and would pretend to be a girl in an online ad if a client were to call the number listed. She was known as the booker. She would verify the client by asking for certain key information and then run that info through certain programs for matches.

Cops love booking prostitution stings through exotic dancer or companionship ads. Everyone we brought on signed a contract that clearly stated she could not participate in any sexual encounters while working with us. So we weren't really tripping on the prostitution, but a good booker still knows how to avoid them. Stings bring down morale.

Some cops took it as a loss (accepted it) when our contractors arrived and simply wrote them a ticket for operating a business without a license, or may have even let them go. Some get the girl alone in a room, stop her from leaving when she doesn't agree to sex immediately, stand between her and the door when she tries to leave, ask for sex again (only now there's a big ass dude between her and the door), and arrest the girl if she agrees. Sounds like an intimidation tactic to me. But I'm just an ex-con, what do I know.

The first night I spent $300 on advertising, worked one contractor, with one booker, and totaled around $2,500 in business. Fuck yeah, marketing. The money was broken up how it needed to be and let's just say I was happy with the end results. I had spent thirteen hours in the office that night/morning, but if the money could stay coming in like that each day, I'd have my initial investment back fast. Shit, I was all for the hours.

While ironworking I'd often look at the other preexisting buildings around us while bolting steel beams to columns. On 90-degree-plus days, at one in the afternoon, with iron dust from grinding metal all day in the sweaty creases of skin behind my neck, I'd spot some fucker drinking a latte and watching me from his air-conditioned office window. I didn't hate that fucker; I wanted to be in the office above that fucker.

I mean why not, right? I didn't know what it was that those people actually did, I just knew they wore suits and didn't need to break their backs in the sun. I was confident I'd appreciate the setting more, and only keep working my way up from there, but in the comfort of air conditioning instead.

Finding reliable contractors did end up being a bitch. Out of fifty calls or emails from applicants, I'd sign on maybe four. To be polite I'll say it was because most didn't have a look we could market. My hiring game was where it needed to be though. The first week I struggled, but after studying my own flaws, I found my flow. At first some contractors would recognize my lack of experience when asking me questions that I know now were basic. But at the time I was clueless.

Speaking with well over fifty girls my first week and only being able to bring on two gave me an opportunity to take notice of where I was losing them in the conversation. I adjusted and learned what girls in the business expected from an agency with each phone interview I had. After the first month I had over ten contractors working with us.

The girls I brought on liked working with us. We didn't make any advances on them, and it almost seemed to shock the girls. I was complimented on my professionalism often, and girls began referring their friends after discovering we were a different kind of agency. I would confidently tell new inquiries that it was our company's goal to make them as much money as possible, keep them happy, feeling safe, and comfortable.

If the owners were always to trying to fuck the girls they work with (literally), that girl would not feel comfortable.

The girl would eventually get over it and start calling other companies. If I got that incoming call, I got that contractor—most of the time anyway.

Once that girl was driven off by her previous agency and then started working with us, she would see the difference immediately. If they were on point (good at what they do), we could have them tripling what they were making at their last company, easily.

20
CHANGES

CHRIS WAS IMPRESSED with my ability to find new contractors and informed me ten hires in a month was pretty fucking good per industry standards. The average norm was one contractor a week before I got there.

The industry has a high turnover rate in regard to the entertainers. So hiring is essential. Chris had a partner at his other company but suspected him of stealing for whatever reason. It was also part of that person's job to hire new contractors, but apparently he sucked at it. Chris began questioning his other partner about his inability to hire all of a sudden. His partner claimed ignorance and said the calls just weren't coming in.

Chris came to sit in on a shift one night and decided to have one of our bookers call his other company's hiring number, just to see if the guy would do his job and pick up the phone at least. What he got was confirmation on his theft suspicions. The guy had started his own mini company from home and was rerouting contractors from his and Chris's company over to his own. Using their company name, and resources, to staff his own personal thing didn't sit well with Chris, to say the least.

They regularly worked with about sixteen girls—a fairly decent number of contractors for a company. While Chris was still processing what had just happened and the information he had been hit with, I did some thinking. From the look of the vein on the side of Chris's head, I could tell the other dude was on his way out and Chris would be parting ways with him soon.

I pitched Chris an idea that came to me and told him it would benefit us both. Split the company down the middle over there and bring his half of the contractors (if they agreed) and office equipment with him to our company.

We'd have eighteen good contractors to regularly work with, two bookers, a heavier advertising budget, more calls, and therefore more profits. Based off the information and totals we obtained throughout the month, combined with Chris's previous tutorials, I knew we could theoretically hit a certain average per month if we were to do the merge. We just needed to continue growing the size of the company. He wouldn't have to assume the full burden of that other company and its responsibilities, and we could share the workload evenly here.

He knew I was reliable and took my money seriously. He also knew I was catching on quick and even excelling at one of the hardest aspects of the business (hiring). Still, he took the night to think it over and decide how to proceed with everything on his plate.

When a new contractor wanted to sign on and work with us, we would schedule an in-person interview. After she submitted a few photos of herself, that is. I call it being Instagrammed when they make it in for the interview, and it becomes clear they have suckered me with filters. It had to be done though. There's too much foul shit going on out there in the world.

This allowed us the opportunity to verify her age by physically checking identifications of the contractors and have paperwork signed agreeing to the company's terms and make sure that she was in fact the girl in the pictures. Interviews for the most part were over in less than fifteen minutes. It just depended on the level of questions the other person had for me. Some agencies will abuse this interview process and try to use it for their own ill-intended sexual purposes.

This was never an option in our interviews. I don't understand how some find it acceptable to abuse a position of authority for their own sexual deviance, regardless of what that line of work may be. Contractors and companies could be equally dependent on each other, if both sides respected each other all the time. But you wouldn't know that by hearing what some of the contractors in this business have to say. Some other agencies would throw out every lie imaginable to manipulate a contractor into choosing their company.

One common lie they'd use is to list all other top agencies in the area to a contractor and claim all those agencies require sex while working and sex for the company owner. The same creep agencies will tell the prospects that other agencies are full of lies and that they will say whatever is needed just to get them in their door. So it creates a "prince of lies" type effect—meaning everything they hear from other agencies, no matter how much sense it makes, could all be lies. So they choose to stay stuck in a situation where they believe the agency they're currently with (flaws included) is the best one out there.

Some contractors experience weeks, months, or even years of abuse before they finally muster the courage to call around. One phone call with me and I'd have them starting that same week, and we would then show them how a real agency operates. We got more calls, had more contractors, and worked hard not only for us, but for them as well. If they weren't happy, we weren't happy.

It wasn't long before the competition started taking notice. Some agencies would often flood my hiring line with bullshit calls in a futile attempt to prevent me from hiring for as long as possible. Others would attempt to distinguish which companionship ads were ours and jam those up as well, in hopes we wouldn't receive calls for the contractors working with us.

The haters failed to realize we had hundreds of ads, and my hiring number was easily changeable. So their treacherous attempts at slowing us down were all for nothing. We had a solid system in place, but a merger with Chris's company would give us both an easier work schedule, and most definitely thicken my pockets.

Chris and I spoke the following afternoon. He had handled things with his partner and informed me he had come to a conclusion on my proposal. He was willing to give my idea a one-month trial run. At the end of the month we would analyze the data collected, and he would make his decision based off those results.

He basically told me, "If you can do what you say you can, I'll make you rich!" At least that's how I took it. A couple weeks into our trial run it was already looking like the merger was almost definite. In two weeks he was making 30 percent more than he had been and was working fewer hours.

The money I had initially invested was already back in my bank account by that point. I was caught up on past due bills and still had money stacking up. I knew I could keep it going if Chris were to decide against it and still be okay. It would take me a little longer to get back to the point we were currently at in our temporary merger, but either way I was confident I could get there and maintain it when I did.

Contractors can be very sneaky at times. Some will begin to steal (in various ways), and you must always be on the lookout for it. Some may try and use sex to further their own agenda. They would do that by trying to lay their game on you in hopes of seducing you—and ultimately getting higher-dollar calls for the most part.

We do the marketing and find clients. We then dispatch those calls to entertainers (contractors) out in the field. Some of the girls figure if they fuck or suck you, you may reserve those higher-dollar calls. But you have to remember one thing before falling for this awesome trickery. Women are psycho. They're awesome, but still psycho.

If you fall for this trick you're fucking up. The contractors all talk with one another. They know when someone gets a high-dollar call. So if a girl who has fucked an owner feels as though she's been put on the back burner, it's all bad.

Enter the psycho. They'll wig out and go on a group texting or social media post frenzy. Or she may try to push you off a yacht. The company as a whole will find out about your sexual encounters with said entertainer, and when she quits (and she will), the other agency she arrives at will know as well. Now your reputation as a professional agency is in jeopardy, and it takes nothing short of a company name change to fix it. Especially if it's a recurring problem, which then wipes away all that effort you put into making your agency name mean something.

I've seen it happen, and I don't fall for it. So the lesson is, don't get high off your own supply people.

The end of our thirty days came, and Chris decided the merger was going well. It was official, we were one company. I had some time to hire so we ended up with twenty-two contractors working with us, eight of which he brought over. We hired another booker and hit it hard.

Even though we had a lighter workload, I still went at it strong. Chris had years in this field and I was just starting. Ninety-hour workweeks were the norm, but I'd basically just nap and live on Java Monsters. When you're in charge of hiring, you got to take the potential contractors' incoming calls, whenever it is they may call.

Getting rich ain't easy. I had spent over seven years in prison for trying once (the wrong way, I know), so I could accept losing some sleep working on it this time around. My back pain would also help keep me up. Sitting too long, lying down too long, or walking too much would bring on muscle spasms in a horrible way.

Dispatching shifts was difficult, but I'd just stay moving around and drowned the pain in as much prescription drugs as I could. I never got too high to function properly or carry on an intelligent conversation while working, but I had pain killers in my system at all times. It was literally the only way I could feel some kind of relief from the otherwise constant pain.

One obstacle I regularly faced while hiring was my accent. I would be frequently asked, "Are you a cholo?" while conducting phone interviews with girls. Some liked it, but most didn't. I found that very frustrating, but it was true. I needed to work on my phone voice. It was a competitive industry. I couldn't afford to keep losing calls because I sounded unprofessional. I worked on sounding as white as I could. Even though I am already white, I still found it difficult to do. Growing up in the hood knocked the white stereotype right out of me.

If ever I ran across an applicant who clearly wasn't going to work, I would log her number in my phone as "do not answer." Then to practice my phone voice, I would wait for the "do not answers" to call in. If I hadn't spoken to them yet, I would proceed to reach deep inside, scrape up my inner David Hasselhoff, subtract the nerdy parts, hit the girl with my usual phone interview process, and then judge their reactions.

After a while I was able to find a "happy place" of how I needed to sound, while also maintaining who I actually was. It did nothing but improve business and helped me in traffic stops big-time. I was still on parole.

Having nothing to hide feels nice, but knowing they can't just pull you out of your car and place you in cuffs during a traffic stop feels even better. So every time I got pulled over, I'd put a little extra icing on the cake and wake David Hasselhoff up for the process.

If I was pulled over when I was first released and questioned by the officer, it almost always resulted in guns being drawn and me being put in cuffs for a while. It was like middle school all over again. They always got spooked when the bank robbery thing came up. But with my new white voice, fancier clothes, and newer model car, I changed all that.

All questions were answered as white as possible during traffic stops, and they were a breeze from then on. Cops wouldn't even bother asking if I was on probation or parole.

Thank you, white privilege, I really enjoy you.

I had never been on a yacht before. The only boat trip of any kind I could even remember was a "Huck Finn" field trip our middle school threw. We went fishing out in the ocean. Now Chris and I were planning a company party and looking at nearby yacht charters. After some thought and company budget planning, we settled on an 85-foot yacht docked in Newport Beach. We'd need a DJ and some catering services on top of the yacht price, but it was in our budget. We allowed everyone to bring a plus one and up to two girlfriends.

We had a full bar, three staterooms, five bathrooms, a crew of five, catering, a DJ, and beautiful women dancing around in low-cut everythings. I've never seen so much ass and titties spilling out at once all around me. Like some sort of competition the girls were having that was snatched straight from heaven.

A couple years ago I had been in the hole, staring out my cell door and only seeing more cells, a gunner, and a sign saying "NO WARNING SHOT" staring back at me. Now I was on a yacht, partying with friends, and a literal boatload of hot chicks, cruising Newport Bay. It felt good. The struggle inside me seemed almost conquered. I was doing everything legal (drugs don't count), and here I was, on a motherfucking yacht staring at these girls snorting cocaine off each other's tits with Three 6 Mafia playing in the background. We favored yachts for company parties after that. No more hungry nights, no more late-night cell raids. Just full steam ahead on mine.

One thing that never went well in the business were ad prices. Depending on how you looked at it, that is. Bigger prices mean smaller agencies can't keep up with our kind of budget. It also meant less immediate profit for us though. I'm not a fan of less immediate profit, so Chris and I talked about that issue and how we could better deal with it, frequently.

We brainstormed and came up with the idea of starting our own website for people to advertise on. The site we were currently using for advertising allowed hyperlinks in the ads we posted. All we had to do was insert a hyperlink to our site when running an ad on theirs and we could redirect the user to our platform. It was almost guaranteed to work. If we could just get a small fraction of what the current site was making, we'd be set for life. In theory anyway.

We agreed that it was worth a shot and settled on the name Freevurse.com.

It would have an adult classifieds section, a firearms section, and a marijuana category among various others. We put the wheels in motion and had construction of the site started within a week. The ads would be free to post in most categories. If a category did require payments for posting an ad on our site, well we had way better prices than anywhere else that we knew of, and we agreed to always keep it that way. For the time being we'd have to keep the main company going strong. Dreams are nice to have, but I'd never lose sight of my reality.

My back pain was ever present, and it took two more years for my surgery to get approved, but afterward, instant relief. I was completely vertical when up and walking after healing from the surgery, and the pain was gone, for the most part. The workdays were still long, but definitely not as difficult. One thing that proved hard to kick without the assistance of the hole was the pain killers. After an overdose on my back patio, I shook that my monkey off my back quickly. I had my sights set on retirement. The site, we figured, may very well lead us to that goal, so we stayed on it.

The links were super effective. We were getting thousands of hits a day every time we would run a hyperlink or marketing campaign. Users started signing up and advertising on the platform. It was slower going than we had originally hoped, but it was making progress and generating some form of revenue. So until Freevurse.com took off, we were stuck using the competition's site.

Unfortunately for us their site would regularly go down for a couple hours a night, constantly raise prices, and were coming under heavy media and political scrutiny for various reasons. One night we went in to open up shop and realized credit card payments were no longer an option on their site. Which meant big problems for some, and great problems for others.

The credit card companies had stopped accepting payments from their platform, and now only something called Bitcoin was a payment option for posting ads. What the fuck was Bitcoin though? We had to find that shit out fast.

Our shift was about to start, and if we didn't find a fix, I was going to hear over two dozen people complain to me at once about getting the night off. Whatever the fuck Bitcoin was, it was going for around $400 apiece. What caught my attention was how it was almost never the same price when I'd go to buy it each time. Bitcoin (symbol BTC) seemed to move like a stock, and it was going up, frequently.

Chris and I both began following the cryptocurrency and watched it steadily rise. It seemed like we had found a new investment opportunity—one that just might speed up my retirement plans.

Freevurse.com was always intended to be for retirement purposes. How long or quickly that retirement may happen is completely up to the users though. Bitcoin seemed a much quicker option.

When we finally got in in 2017, BTC was super low compared to today's price, in the hundreds. But the growth seemed crazy on this thing. Although its price was soaring into the thousands, pricey, Bitcoin allowed you the option of buying only fractions of a coin, and your investment would grow accordingly.

Crypto coins are used as a store of value by some, for trading by others, and a money transfer system by all. This digital record called blockchain technology also makes counterfeiting existing coins impossible. It's the fucking future.

Now I'm no expert on Bitcoin or Litecoin (LTC), but I know it makes money. Some call it a bubble and say it will pop as the dot.com bubble did in the early 2000s. But if you made your way out of that bubble before it popped, you were a rich individual. Again I'm no expert, but as long as you can get out at the right time, you're good either way. If you set a stop loss (a price you set to sell holdings and avoid major losses), you can't lose, in my opinion.

Trading in cryptocurrency is legal, consistent money (if you learn how to trade), and you can work from your phone. From wherever the fuck you feel like working. No ceiling can limit you, only nerves will.

You start off with what you can afford, pay attention to the news and charts, distinguish patterns and what may cause them (using charts and Google is easiest), and trade what you can. You'll keep stacking coin ($) every time you make a good trade. Each coin has a different valuation usually based on its market cap (amount of coins available), functionality, and transaction rate.

I don't have all my eggs in one crypto basket. I'm no crypto expert. I'm just working with what I got, while it's available. Once you hit a comfortable figure, shift some of the profits toward a new enterprise. I co-own our online classifieds site (Freevurse.com) and an escort consulting business (Hundredsandfifties.com) where I give any woman or agencies, or start-ups, advice on how to grow their business.

Funny, isn't it? I did time for robbing banks. Now we don't need banks. I'm stacking coin. And I'm still walking away with piles of cash.

21
IN IT TO WIN IT

I WAS LET off parole in late 2012, shortly after our merger was finalized. I had no more worries of being randomly sent back to prison on a bogus parole violation, and no more concerns of the ISU kicking in my door with the PO (parole officer).

I was once with a guy serving a one-year parole violation because his son had a cap gun (with orange tip) in his toy chest. The parole board called it a weapon and gave him a year because he was a two-striker. The district attorney didn't press charges (obviously), but the CCPOA demanded a sacrifice, so off to prison he went for a full year of his life, tucked safely away from society. Cap-gun-possessing motherfucker. Not on our streets.

California parole officers may search wherever they please if it's your house, or if you have access to those areas. An unlocked but closed door didn't matter; you're considered to have access. His kid's door was unlocked.

My mom owned two or three firearms, and I could have gotten life in prison if she had forgotten to close her safe and the PO had decided to stop by. So when I got off parole, it was definitely a breath of fresh air. I stayed living in my Lakewood one-bedroom apartment for a couple years after starting my business. I could have easily afforded better living conditions, but I chose to stack up cash before I started making any big purchases.

It took me years to even decide to finally pay for cable services. I only caved to that because my girlfriend was nagging me about it. What's HBO to a boss, right? I stayed looking sharp though, had cash, ate whatever I wanted, had a roof over my head, nice car, and just watched my net worth blow up (increase in volume) each day. No unneeded distractions or expenses.

Cruising down the Pacific Coast Highway was an enjoyment of mine. I would jump on in Long Beach and drive down to Dana Point, then back up again. Passing Newport Beach was always the highlight of the trip. It's a beautiful area with gorgeous scenery and expensive homes, stretched out across even more expensive strips of sand. A no-drama kind of city. The kind of spot I had always dreamed of living in. I cruised that same path since I had been released. Always telling myself I'd live there some day.

Today, I live in a cool spot by the bay in beautiful Newport Beach, California. Doing the family thing with my girl. I never go hungry, and if I do, it was my own fault for slipping (allowing it to happen). I wear nice watches and clothes, drive a nice car, always have money, donate to charity—and I always remember I came from Otay. I live by another body of water now, and they haven't found one dead person or pieces thereof the whole time I've been here.

But I remember who I am. I grew up struggling, have twenty-some felony convictions pertaining to bank robbery, two strikes, been harassed just for walking to the store, spent my years in the system, and have seen their corruption firsthand. I went through their soulless machine and came out on top.

I'm looking at this book as an instructional guide for my readers on how to potentially avoid crime and still be able to pay your bills. I want to help people get the fuck out of whatever situation they're in and get them in a better one. Whether you're doing great already, or have seen better days, this is how I did it, and these are how things lined up for me in life. If I had not gone to prison, and had chosen to instead focus on learning more about computers and programming, I would most definitely be better off than I am today.

Those years set me back in a real way, and for nothing but a few months of fun and partying.

Avoid falling into the same trap I and so many others have. Expand your friend circle. Instead of being surrounded by criminals and depression or telling gangster-ass prison stories to your little cousins or brothers when you get out so they learn to idolize the gangster life, try not to get into the life. The system is designed to take the people in the hood down and keep them down.

I'm electing to rise like my Corona when I put the salt in. The best revenge in my opinion is success. Put them out of work by winning the game. Then sit back and laugh.

The criminal justice system wants you off the street and into prison where they make money keeping you there. Do you want to die in prison? Sometimes the guards will make that decision for you. Maybe the homies can do it for you if you fuck up, and you'll be another trail of yard blood on the track.

I'm not saying you should completely change who you are as a person (although we could all use some work). Good people can do bad shit when necessary. Just stop for a moment and look at the future no matter where you find yourself and think about what it could be like to make that change. Fucking envision it.

As far as my vision goes, I'm almost there. I always set my goals to extreme levels. I'm no multimillionaire, but I'm working on it, believe that shit. I'm just trying to make a dollar out of fifteen cents and continue to live life right. I believe in second chances for those who truly want it.

I've lost my right to bear arms in California, but I'm a strong gun supporter. I've been locked up with people who just went out one day, started killing people, and got hooked on it until their capture. So yeah, you should definitely be able to blow those motherfuckers away no problem if they come crawling in on you one night. The walls would need to be cleaned either way, but if you had a gun, at least it'll be you doing the cleaning, instead of a team of crime scene investigators moving you out of the way first to get some more pics, you know?

If you are not, or have never been, a member of the neighborhood struggle club and therefore cannot relate to my frustrations, then I apologize for the long rant and hope you've enjoyed my story either way.

Shit started going well for me because I had immediate help from my mom upon my release from prison. If I hadn't had her there when I got out, and was instead solely reliant on the system to "help" me get on track, I'd most likely be writing a kite in the SHU and not this book right now.

Everybody needs help at some point, fucking everybody. If you're ever in a position to help someone out and it costs you nothing to do so, fucking do it. Hold that door open for the person coming up behind you at the bank. But like the FBI told me once I'd signed my deal, "Just because you held the door open for people doesn't make you a nice person. You were there to rob the bank!"

They're right. So what I'm saying is help people out, but don't proceed to fuck them over. Function in society and make that first step to success. Get the fuck out of the system and stay out, *please*.

Meet me out on Newport Bay. You'll see me coming too, don't trip. I'll be the guy in a 100-foot yacht blaring 2Pac, with a tattooed jersey on my back. Last name South Side, sporting number 15. Just counting my coin and hysterically laughing at all my haters. Sipping on a glass of that good shit. Coming to a dock near you, people. Stay up, and stay hustling. Peace.

ACKNOWLEDGMENTS

ABOVE ALL ELSE I'd like to thank my family. Despite all the bullshit and stress I put them through, they stayed loving me unconditionally and never lost hope. I wouldn't have been able to do it without you all being there. Your support was always on my mind at my worst time and helped me push my way through it. I love you all and I truly thank you for everything you've done, and for always being there.

To Crystal Summers, my longtime friend who visited me in prison, and who is now my girlfriend, thank you for being there. And to her daughter, Amyra, whom I hope doesn't read this till she's forty, you rock.

I'd also like to thank the good people of Otay, California. The strength and resilience of that community and its residents is a thing of beauty. The neighborhood pride and loyalty I experienced while growing up helped me not only prepare for one of the most difficult times in my life, but helped get me all the way through it. Nothing but Otay love, baby.

To my editor, Sandra Wendel. You really know what you're doing. This story wouldn't be the same without you and your skills.

I'd like to thank all the good homies from the South out there. Don't think you're all forgotten. To the older homies, thank you for everything you've done to put it down in there and make it easier on the younger homies entering the system. To those that were with me and those that I haven't met, thank you for having my back and trusting me to have yours. *Mis saludos y respetos a todos. Y un chingo de gracias!*

I'd like to thank all the members of the ISU. You kept me on my toes. Without you and your illegal "policing" techniques to use as stepping stones, I wouldn't be where I am today. Standing on a mountain built of your own corruption, pissing down in your

Cheerios. You're the best. Just remember to let Flowers out of his shoebox for air, okay, you guys. Little guy probably gets lonely.

To my cats Tiny and Blink. Thank you for constantly walking on my keyboard throughout the entire process of writing this book and for rubbing your fur across my face on those summer days. Couldn't have done it without you.

Finally, thank you to my readers. If you've got this far, you must have liked my story and I appreciate you. Unless you're a rat. If you're a rat, you can suck a dick.

ABOUT THE AUTHOR

RICHARD STANLEY WAS raised in a lower income area of South San Diego. Although he was a high school dropout, he obtained a business degree as a serial entrepreneur—in bank robbery.

As acknowledgment of his work in the banking industry, he was graciously accepted into an institution of higher education operated by the California state prison system to further his studies in the criminal justice field with a full-ride scholarship for no less than seven years, out of a possible eight.

During his tenure at the Donovan campus, he specialized in a course in hustling and earned an informal degree in procuring life's necessities and wilderness survival skills. For his efforts, he was rewarded with a sabbatical of sorts and was allowed seven months of personal time in solitude for reflection to just appreciate life. He was off the grid, so to speak, and not allowed cell phones, laptops, or even eating utensils at times. Although Stanley initially declined the retreat time, the institution insisted he spend time in a remote part of campus.

Because most employers would not recognize his degree in higher education, Stanley found it difficult to obtain employment in any field once he left his educational institution. He eventually became an ironworker until he was sidelined with an injury.

Using his entrepreneurial skills and exclusive state-funded education, he developed more conventional ways to hustle and currently serves as a consultant to business leaders on the adult marketing world and is co-owner of the online classified website, freevurse.com.

He also has become a day trader in Bitcoin and Litecoin because he has vowed to never rob a bank again, and now with cryptocurrency, he will never need a bank again.

Stanley lives in Newport Beach, California, with his girlfriend and her daughter. He enjoys the finest marijuana and excellent Southern California red wine.

PRISON: WHERE RIGHT AND WRONG FLIPPED UPSIDE DOWN

Want more inside prison stories? Read next—

"Richard Stanley is by far one of the most fascinating people I've ever interviewed," says Adam Carolla, host of the #1 Daily Downloaded Podcast in the World

"We were expected to obey outside world laws while living in an element of depravity that was almost purely primal."

As prisoner T-83401 in the California prison system, convicted bank robber Richard Stanley survived seven years living in a subculture all its own. This is the inside story of the ways of the California prison world—

- Where prison guards ruled and where smuggling, contraband, escape, and drugs meant survival or surrender to a system that perpetuated itself,

- Where prison guards turned simple sentences into life behind bars and even killed over a misunderstanding or sent the unruly to the "hole," never to be heard from again (Stanley spent seven months in isolation for smuggling in Hawaiian Punch),

- Where right and wrong flipped upside down, and

- Why the prison system—with little hope of reform and rehabilitation—has become the LinkedIn.com of the criminal world.

For more info, visit the book's website: www.UpOnGameBook.com. Available on Amazon in paperback, ebook, and audiobook.

Made in the USA
Middletown, DE
23 January 2022